The content of this book is based on various sources and is intended for educational and entertainment purposes only. While the author has made every effort to ensure the accuracy, completeness, and reliability of the information provided, the information may be subject to errors, omissions, or inaccuracies. Therefore, the author makes no warranties, express or implied, regarding the content of this book.

Readers are advised to seek the guidance of a licensed professional before attempting any techniques or actions outlined in this book. The author is not responsible for any losses, damages, or injuries that may arise from the use of information contained within. The information provided in this book is not intended to be a substitute for professional advice, and readers should not rely solely on the information presented.

By reading this book, readers acknowledge that the author is not providing legal, financial, medical, or professional advice. Any reliance on the information contained in this book is solely at the reader's own risk.

Thank you for selecting this book as a valuable source of knowledge and inspiration. Our aim is to provide you with insights and information that will enrich your understanding and enhance your personal growth. We appreciate your decision to embark on this journey of discovery with us, and we hope that this book will exceed your expectations and leave a lasting impact on your life.

Title: The Dawn of Chaos: The Fall of Eastern Han and the Rise of the Three Kingdoms

Subtitle: Power Struggles, Betrayals, and the Birth of Rival Kingdoms

Series: The Three Kingdoms Unveiled: A Comprehensive Journey through Ancient China

Author: Jonathan T. Morgan

Table of Contents

Introduction

Setting the Stage: The Decline of the Eastern Han Dynasty

The Eastern Han Dynasty, which ruled China for nearly two centuries, had experienced a glorious period of stability and prosperity under the reign of Emperor Wu. However, as the Han Dynasty reached its later years, a series of internal and external factors began to erode its foundations, leading to its eventual decline and the fragmentation of the empire.

At the dawn of the 2nd century CE, the Eastern Han Dynasty faced mounting challenges that would test its ability to maintain control over its vast territories. The economy, once thriving due to agricultural advancements and flourishing trade along the Silk Road, started to falter. Agricultural production declined, leading to food shortages and the suffering of the peasant population. These hardships were exacerbated by natural disasters such as floods and droughts, which further strained the already fragile economy.

Simultaneously, the Han court faced internal struggles for power. Eunuchs, who held significant influence in the imperial court, engaged in political intrigue and corruption, undermining the authority of the emperor and fostering an atmosphere of mistrust. The eunuchs' unchecked power and their manipulation of the imperial succession led to instability and further weakened the central government.

The decline of the Eastern Han Dynasty was also marked by regional uprisings and rebellions that challenged its authority. One of the most significant of these was the Yellow Turban Rebellion, which erupted in 184 CE. Led by the Taoist healer Zhang Jue and his brothers, the rebellion capitalized on the discontent among the rural population, promising a utopian society and relief from the hardships they endured. The rebellion rapidly spread across the empire, sowing chaos and threatening the very foundations of Han rule.

The court's response to the rebellion was marred by indecisiveness and internal divisions. Multiple factions vied for control, leading to a fragmented response and an inability to effectively quell the rebellion. While the Han Dynasty managed to suppress the Yellow Turban Rebellion, the conflict exposed the deep-seated issues that plagued the empire and served as a catalyst for further turmoil.

In addition to internal challenges, the Eastern Han Dynasty faced external threats from nomadic tribes on the northern borders. These tribes, such as the Xiongnu and later the Xianbei, frequently raided Han territories, further straining the empire's resources and military capabilities.

As the empire became increasingly fragmented and weakened, powerful warlords emerged, seizing control of vast territories and establishing their own fiefdoms. These warlords, known as "doujun," operated as quasi-independent rulers, challenging the authority of the Han Dynasty and further contributing to the disintegration of centralized power.

The decline of the Eastern Han Dynasty and the subsequent rise of the Three Kingdoms were not sudden events but rather the result of a gradual erosion of political, economic, and social stability. The seeds of division were sown, setting the stage for the tumultuous era that would follow.

In the chapters that follow, we will explore the key events, major figures, and political dynamics that unfolded during the Three Kingdoms period. We will delve into the rise of the Kingdoms of Wei, Shu, and Wu, examining their leaders, conflicts, and ultimate fate. By presenting a balanced historical narrative, we aim to shed light on this transformative era in Chinese history and its enduring legacy.

Chapter 1: The Fragmented Empire

The Seeds of Division: Factors Leading to the Rise of Three Kingdoms

The Three Kingdoms period in China's history was a turbulent era characterized by political fragmentation and incessant warfare. It emerged as a result of a culmination of factors and underlying tensions that had been brewing during the later years of the Eastern Han Dynasty. In this chapter, we will explore the seeds of division that paved the way for the rise of the Three Kingdoms—Wei, Shu, and Wu.

1. Economic Challenges and Agrarian Crisis

The economic foundation of the Eastern Han Dynasty, which had once flourished under Emperor Wu, began to show signs of strain as the dynasty progressed. The Han Dynasty's reliance on agriculture as the backbone of its economy faced multiple challenges. Land distribution issues, unequal tax burdens, and corrupt local officials led to a widening wealth gap and social unrest. The agrarian crisis was further exacerbated by natural disasters, including floods and droughts, which disrupted agricultural production and caused widespread famine. These economic hardships created fertile ground for discontent and resentment among the populace.

1. Political Instability and Court Intrigue

The political landscape of the Eastern Han Dynasty was marked by internal power struggles and court intrigue. The eunuchs, who wielded considerable influence within the imperial court, engaged in political manipulation and corruption, undermining the authority of the emperor. Their interference in the selection of emperors and control over key positions weakened the central government and eroded public trust. This power struggle at the court level hindered effective governance and left the dynasty vulnerable to external and internal challenges.

2. Regionalism and Warlordism

As the central authority of the Han Dynasty weakened, regionalism and warlordism gained prominence. Local military commanders, known as warlords or "doujun," took advantage of the central government's diminishing control to establish their own power bases. These warlords controlled vast territories and maintained their own armies, challenging the authority of the imperial court. Their actions further contributed to the fragmentation of the empire and created a climate of constant power struggles and shifting allegiances.

3. Ethnic Tensions and Frontier Threats

The Eastern Han Dynasty faced persistent threats from nomadic tribes along its northern borders, particularly the Xiongnu and later the Xianbei. These nomadic groups frequently raided Han territories, causing significant damage and straining the empire's resources. The Han Dynasty's inability to effectively manage these frontier challenges led to ethnic tensions and a growing sense of insecurity among the populace. The perception that the central government was unable to protect its subjects further eroded its legitimacy and contributed to the disintegration of the empire.

4. Intellectual and Cultural Transformations

The Three Kingdoms period coincided with significant intellectual and cultural transformations. The emergence of Daoism, Confucianism, and Buddhism offered alternative philosophies and spiritual beliefs that resonated with a population disillusioned by the decline of the Han Dynasty. Intellectuals and scholars sought solace in these new ideologies, contributing to a cultural shift that questioned traditional authority and promoted individualism. These philosophical and cultural changes further undermined the centralized power of the Han Dynasty and laid the groundwork for the rise of regional powers.

Conclusion

The seeds of division that ultimately led to the rise of the Three Kingdoms were sown during the later years of the Eastern Han Dynasty. Economic challenges, political instability, regionalism, ethnic tensions, and cultural transformations all played significant roles in creating an environment ripe for fragmentation and conflict. These factors intertwined and interacted with one another, creating a complex web of dynamics that shaped the destiny of China during the Three Kingdoms period.

In the following chapters, we will delve deeper into the key figures and events that unfolded during this era, examining the rise to power, conflicts, and ultimate fate of the Wei, Shu, and Wu kingdoms. By presenting a comprehensive overview of this transformative period in Chinese history, we aim to provide readers with a balanced understanding of the political, social, and cultural forces that shaped the Three Kingdoms.

A Glimpse of the Three Kingdoms Era: Key Figures and Themes

The Three Kingdoms period stands as one of the most captivating and iconic periods in Chinese history. It was a time of great upheaval, where the once-unified empire of the Han Dynasty splintered into three distinct kingdoms: Wei, Shu, and Wu. This chapter provides a glimpse into the Three Kingdoms era, highlighting key figures and themes that shaped this transformative period.

1. The Heroic Figures

The Three Kingdoms period was characterized by a multitude of larger-than-life figures whose exploits and legacies continue to captivate audiences to this day. Among them, we find remarkable individuals such as Cao Cao, Liu Bei, and Sun Quan, who rose to prominence amidst the chaos and carved their names into the annals of history. Cao Cao, the cunning and ambitious warlord, sought to unify China under his rule. Liu Bei, the virtuous and benevolent leader, aspired to establish a kingdom that upheld righteousness and justice. Sun Quan, the shrewd strategist, maneuvered to secure his kingdom's position and expand its influence. These figures, with their distinct personalities, ambitions, and strategies, played pivotal roles in the Three Kingdoms era.

2. Themes of Brotherhood and Loyalty

One of the enduring themes that emerged from the Three Kingdoms period is that of brotherhood and loyalty. The Oath of the Peach Garden, a legendary event where Liu Bei, Guan Yu, and Zhang Fei swore an oath of loyalty and brotherhood, exemplifies the deep bonds forged amidst the chaos. Loyalty to one's lord and brotherhood among sworn brothers became central tenets, influencing the actions of key figures and their subordinates. The Three Kingdoms era witnessed remarkable displays of loyalty, sacrifice, and camaraderie, as exemplified by Zhuge Liang's unwavering devotion to Liu Bei and the brotherly bond between Guan Yu and Zhang Fei.

3. Strategic Brilliance and Military Conflicts

The Three Kingdoms era was marked by intense military conflicts and strategic brilliance. Cao Cao, renowned for his military acumen, devised intricate plans and successfully navigated the complex landscape of warfare. The Battle of Guandu, a decisive engagement between Cao Cao and Yuan Shao, showcased his strategic brilliance and marked a turning point in the balance of power. The Battle of Red Cliffs, a legendary naval confrontation, saw the combined forces of Liu Bei and Sun Quan successfully repel Cao Cao's mighty army. These battles, along with numerous other engagements, highlight the intricate strategies, tactical maneuvers, and martial prowess displayed by the key figures of the Three Kingdoms.

4. Political Intrigues and Betrayals

In the midst of warfare and military campaigns, the Three Kingdoms era was rife with political intrigues and betrayals. Ambitious figures vied for power and influence, leading to shifting alliances and treachery. The Shu-Wu Alliance, initially formed to counter the might of Cao Cao's Wei, faced internal tensions and betrayals that strained the partnership. Zhuge Liang's legendary Northern Expeditions, intended to conquer Wei, were hindered by internal conflicts and shifting loyalties among his own ranks. The Three Kingdoms era witnessed not only grand battles but also intricate webs of political machinations and the consequences of trust and betrayal.

5. Cultural and Literary Legacy

The Three Kingdoms period left an indelible mark on Chinese culture and literature. One of the most influential literary works to emerge from this era is the "Romance of the Three Kingdoms," attributed to the renowned author Luo Guanzhong. This epic historical novel, while blending fact and fiction, immortalized the heroes, the conflicts, and the intricate political landscape of the Three Kingdoms. The

"Romance of the Three Kingdoms" has since become an iconic piece of literature, inspiring countless adaptations in various art forms and shaping popular perceptions of the era.

Conclusion

The Three Kingdoms era remains an enduring source of fascination, captivating audiences with its dynamic characters, epic battles, and intricate political maneuverings. The heroic figures, themes of brotherhood and loyalty, strategic brilliance, political intrigues, and cultural legacy collectively contribute to the allure of this transformative period in Chinese history. In the following chapters, we will delve deeper into the stories and experiences of these key figures, explore their rise to power, conflicts, and ultimate fate, and further unravel the complex tapestry of the Three Kingdoms era.

Chapter 1: The Fragmented Empire

The Yellow Turban Rebellion: Catalyst for Crisis

The early years of the Three Kingdoms period were marked by a series of events that shook the foundations of the Eastern Han Dynasty, leading to its eventual fragmentation. Among these events, the Yellow Turban Rebellion emerged as a significant catalyst for the ensuing crisis. In this chapter, we will explore the origins, motivations, and impact of the Yellow Turban Rebellion, which ignited a wave of chaos and set the stage for the division of China.

1. The Socioeconomic Climate of the Late Eastern Han Dynasty

Before delving into the Yellow Turban Rebellion itself, it is crucial to understand the socioeconomic climate that laid the groundwork for such a widespread uprising. The Eastern Han Dynasty, once a prosperous empire, had been grappling with various challenges that created discontent among the population. Unequal land distribution, heavy taxation, corruption, and rising social inequality all contributed to a sense of frustration and disillusionment among the peasants and common people. These underlying socioeconomic tensions would prove fertile ground for the seeds of rebellion.

2. The Emergence of the Yellow Turban Movement

The Yellow Turban Rebellion was initially sparked by the activities of Zhang Jue and his two brothers, Zhang Bao and Zhang Liang. The Zhang brothers, claiming to be divine healers and prophets, formed a messianic movement known as the Yellow Turbans. They preached a doctrine of social equality, promising salvation and relief from the hardships faced by the common people. The Yellow Turban Movement gained rapid popularity, attracting followers from all walks of life who were disillusioned with the existing social order.

3. Ideology and Organization of the Yellow Turbans

The Yellow Turban Rebellion was not merely a spontaneous outburst of discontent but a well-organized movement with its own ideology and structure. The Yellow Turbans advocated a blend of religious and egalitarian principles, emphasizing the importance of communal ownership of land and shared wealth. They organized their followers into units called "bands" and established a hierarchical structure with regional leaders and military commanders. This organizational framework allowed the rebellion to coordinate its actions and pose a significant challenge to the imperial authority.

4. The Outbreak and Spread of the Rebellion

In the year 184 CE, the Yellow Turban Rebellion erupted in several provinces simultaneously. The rebellion quickly gained momentum, drawing in vast numbers of disaffected peasants, tenant farmers, and even some members of the gentry. Armed with their distinctive yellow headbands, the Yellow Turbans launched attacks on government officials, local landlords, and anyone associated with the oppressive social order. The rebellion spread like wildfire, engulfing multiple regions and posing a grave threat to the stability of the Eastern Han Dynasty.

5. The Imperial Response and Military Campaigns

The Yellow Turban Rebellion presented a severe challenge to the authority of the Eastern Han Dynasty. Initially caught off guard by the scale and ferocity of the uprising, the imperial court mobilized its forces to suppress the rebellion. The court dispatched various military commanders, including Liu Bei, Cao Cao, and Sun Jian, to quell the rebellion in different regions. These military campaigns against the Yellow Turbans were met with varying degrees of success, with the rebellion proving resilient and difficult to extinguish completely.

6. Long-Term Impact and Significance

While the Yellow Turban Rebellion was eventually suppressed by the imperial forces, its consequences reverberated throughout the Three Kingdoms period. The rebellion exposed the deep-rooted social and economic issues plaguing the empire, highlighting the urgent need for reform. It also demonstrated the weaknesses of the central authority and exposed the fragmentation of power among regional warlords. The Yellow Turban Rebellion was a pivotal event that shattered the illusion of a unified empire and set the stage for the subsequent power struggles and conflicts that defined the Three Kingdoms era.

Conclusion

The Yellow Turban Rebellion was a turning point in the history of the Eastern Han Dynasty, signaling the beginning of its decline and fragmentation. This mass uprising, fueled by socioeconomic grievances and led by the Yellow Turban Movement, exposed the underlying tensions within the empire and set in motion a series of events that would shape the Three Kingdoms era. In the chapters that follow, we will explore the power struggles, rise of key figures, and the ultimate fate of the Three Kingdoms as the empire descended into chaos and division.

Warlords and Local Fiefdoms: Power Struggles Amidst Chaos

As the Yellow Turban Rebellion subsided, China found itself plunged into a state of profound instability. The central authority of the Eastern Han Dynasty had weakened significantly, creating a power vacuum that led to the rise of warlords and the emergence of local fiefdoms. This chapter explores the dynamics of power struggles amidst the chaos, as ambitious figures vied for control and established their own domains in the fragmented empire.

1. The Erosion of Central Authority

The aftermath of the Yellow Turban Rebellion saw the erosion of the Eastern Han Dynasty's central authority. The rebellion had exposed the dynasty's inability to maintain order and effectively govern the vast territory it once controlled. Local officials and military commanders began asserting greater autonomy, exploiting the power vacuum and asserting control over their respective regions. The weakening grip of the central authority created a fragmented landscape where warlords and regional powers rose to prominence.

2. The Rise of Regional Warlords

The power struggles that ensued amidst the chaos of the fragmented empire gave birth to numerous regional warlords who sought to consolidate their power and expand their influence. These warlords, often military commanders or influential figures in their respective regions, leveraged their military prowess, strategic alliances, and political maneuverings to carve out their own territories. Figures such as Yuan Shao, Liu Biao, and Zhang Xiu emerged as formidable warlords, commanding significant resources and vying for dominance in the new political landscape.

3. Military Campaigns and Territorial Expansion

The power struggles among warlords manifested in a series of military campaigns and territorial expansions. Ambitious warlords sought to increase their domains and consolidate their power by conquering neighboring territories or subjugating rival warlords. Battles such as the Battle of Changban, where Liu Bei clashed with Cao Cao's forces, or the conflicts between Yuan Shao and Gongsun Zan, exemplified the intense rivalries and territorial ambitions that characterized this period. These military campaigns were not only driven by the desire for power but also shaped by personal grudges, strategic considerations, and the pursuit of resources.

4. The Establishment of Local Fiefdoms

As warlords solidified their control over territories, they began establishing local fiefdoms as a means of asserting their authority and consolidating their rule. These fiefdoms operated as semi-autonomous regions, with warlords acting as de facto rulers. They appointed their own officials, collected taxes, administered justice, and maintained their own military forces. The establishment of local fiefdoms further fragmented the empire, with each warlord consolidating power within their respective domains.

5. Alliances, Betrayals, and Shifting Loyalties

In the ever-shifting landscape of power struggles, alliances were forged and betrayed with remarkable frequency. Warlords sought to secure their positions and gain strategic advantages by forming alliances or marriages, only to betray their allies when advantageous. Figures like Sun Ce, the founder of the Kingdom of Wu, demonstrated the intricate dance of forming and breaking alliances to further their own interests. Shifting loyalties among generals, advisors, and officials added another layer of complexity to the power struggles, as individuals sought to align themselves with the rising powers or protect their own positions.

6. The Impact on the Civilian Population

Amidst the power struggles and conflicts, it was the civilian population that bore the brunt of the chaos. The common people experienced the hardships of warfare, with their lives disrupted by frequent battles, plundering, and the imposition of heavy taxation. Local economies suffered as resources were diverted towards military campaigns, and the breakdown of law and order led to increased banditry and social unrest. The plight of the civilian population during this period underscores the grim realities of the power struggles and fragmentation of the empire.

Conclusion

The period following the Yellow Turban Rebellion witnessed the rise of warlords and the fragmentation of the Eastern Han Dynasty. Power struggles, territorial expansions, and the establishment of local fiefdoms defined the chaotic landscape of the era. The actions of ambitious warlords, their alliances, and shifting loyalties shaped the destiny of the empire and laid the groundwork for the subsequent rise of the Three Kingdoms. In the chapters to come, we will delve further into the individual warlords, their ambitions, and the conflicts that shaped the Three Kingdoms period.

The Abdication of Emperor Xian: The Official Split

The fragmentation of the Eastern Han Dynasty reached its culmination with the abdication of Emperor Xian, marking the official split of the empire into three distinct kingdoms: Wei, Shu, and Wu. This pivotal event in Chinese history had far-reaching consequences and set the stage for the power struggles and conflicts that defined the Three Kingdoms era. In this chapter, we will explore the circumstances leading to Emperor Xian's abdication, the key players involved, and the implications of the official split.

1. Emperor Xian and the Crisis of Legitimacy

Emperor Xian, born Liu Xie, ascended to the throne at a young age and reigned as the nominal ruler of the Eastern Han Dynasty. However, his reign was characterized by a lack of real power, as influential eunuchs and warlords exerted control over the imperial court. Emperor Xian faced a crisis of legitimacy, as his authority was continually undermined by factions vying for power. The weaknesses of his reign laid the groundwork for the fragmentation of the empire.

2. Dong Zhuo and the Capturing of the Capital

Dong Zhuo, a powerful warlord and minister, played a pivotal role in the events leading to the abdication of Emperor Xian. Seeking to consolidate his power, Dong Zhuo seized control of the imperial capital, Luoyang, and held

Emperor Xian hostage. Under Dong Zhuo's control, the imperial court became a puppet of his regime, further eroding the central authority and legitimacy of the Han Dynasty.

3. The Coalition Against Dong Zhuo

The tyrannical rule of Dong Zhuo sparked widespread opposition among regional warlords and officials who sought to remove him from power. A coalition was formed, led by influential figures such as Yuan Shao, Cao Cao, and Sun Jian, with the goal of liberating Emperor Xian and restoring order to the empire. The coalition launched military campaigns against Dong Zhuo's forces, culminating in the Battle of Guandu, where Cao Cao emerged victorious. The successful coalition against Dong Zhuo demonstrated the potential for regional powers to challenge the central authority and set the stage for further divisions.

4. The Shift of Power: Cao Cao's Influence

With Dong Zhuo's removal from power, Cao Cao emerged as one of the most influential figures in the empire. Recognizing the weakening central authority, Cao Cao sought to establish his own power base and gain control over Emperor Xian. Through strategic maneuvering and military victories, Cao Cao effectively controlled the emperor, positioning himself as the de facto ruler of the empire. This shift of power and Cao Cao's growing influence paved the way for the subsequent division of the empire.

5. Emperor Xian's Abdication and the Division of the Empire

Under the influence of Cao Cao, Emperor Xian was coerced into abdicating the throne, officially splitting the empire into three kingdoms. Cao Cao established the Kingdom of Wei, with its capital at Xuchang, becoming its de facto ruler. Liu Bei, a regional warlord, declared himself the Emperor of Shu Han, establishing the Kingdom of Shu with its capital at Chengdu. Meanwhile, Sun Quan founded the Kingdom of Wu in the southeastern region, with its capital at Jianye. The abdication of Emperor Xian marked the beginning of the Three Kingdoms era, with each kingdom vying for supremacy and embarking on their own paths of political and military conquest.

6. Implications and Consequences

The official split of the empire had profound implications for the balance of power, political dynamics, and the subsequent conflicts that defined the Three Kingdoms period. The division solidified the independent rule of each kingdom, creating a tripartite struggle for dominance that would shape the next several decades. It also represented a symbolic shift in the perception of political legitimacy, as regional warlords now held the reins of power, challenging the traditional central authority of the imperial throne.

Conclusion

The abdication of Emperor Xian and the official split of the Eastern Han Dynasty marked a definitive turning point in Chinese history. The weakness of Emperor Xian's reign, the rise of influential warlords like Dong Zhuo and Cao Cao, and the subsequent division of the empire set the stage for the power struggles, conflicts, and political dynamics that characterized the Three Kingdoms era. In the chapters that follow, we will delve deeper into the rise of the individual kingdoms, the key figures involved, and the battles that shaped their destinies.

Chapter 2: Cao Cao and the Kingdom of Wei

Rise of Cao Cao: From Military Commander to Imperial Advisor

Cao Cao, a central figure in the Three Kingdoms period, played a pivotal role in the establishment and rise of the Kingdom of Wei. From his beginnings as a military commander to his eventual position as an influential imperial advisor, Cao Cao's ascent to power was marked by strategic brilliance, political maneuvering, and military successes. This chapter explores the rise of Cao Cao, his early life and career, and the key events that propelled him towards becoming one of the most influential figures of his time.

1. Early Life and Background

Cao Cao was born in 155 CE into a family of modest means, but with a lineage connected to the imperial court. His father, Cao Song, held a low-ranking position in the government. From an early age, Cao Cao exhibited intelligence, ambition, and a thirst for knowledge. He received a classical education and demonstrated exceptional talent in literature, military strategy, and governance.

2. Military Achievements and the Yellow Turban Rebellion

Cao Cao's military career began during the chaotic period following the Yellow Turban Rebellion. Recognizing the need for stability and order, Cao Cao formed a volunteer army and actively participated in campaigns against the rebel forces. His successes in suppressing the rebellion and restoring peace to the region earned him recognition and a growing reputation as a capable military commander.

3. The Battle of Guandu: Cao Cao's Consolidation of Power

One of the defining moments in Cao Cao's rise to power was the Battle of Guandu in 200 CE. Facing off against his rival Yuan Shao, Cao Cao's forces emerged victorious, securing his control over the central plains of China. The battle showcased Cao Cao's strategic genius and military prowess, solidifying his position as a formidable warlord and paving the way for his further expansion.

4. Establishing the Xuchang Administration

With his power base in the central plains, Cao Cao established the Xuchang Administration, effectively governing the territories under his control. He implemented a series of reforms aimed at promoting agricultural development, improving infrastructure, and consolidating his rule. Cao Cao's administration demonstrated his administrative abilities and his focus on fostering stability and prosperity within his domain.

5. Cao Cao's Pursuit of the Emperor: A Bid for Legitimacy

Seeking to enhance his own legitimacy and consolidate his power, Cao Cao embarked on a campaign to bring Emperor Xian, the nominal ruler of the Eastern Han Dynasty, under his control. Through political maneuvering and military pressure, Cao Cao convinced Emperor Xian to move the capital from Chang'an to Xuchang, effectively placing the emperor within his grasp. While maintaining the veneer of loyalty to the Han Dynasty, Cao Cao effectively became the de facto ruler, positioning himself as an imperial advisor and consolidating his authority.

6. Governance and Reforms

Cao Cao's rule over the Kingdom of Wei was marked by his focus on governance and reforms. He implemented policies aimed at strengthening the central authority, promoting economic development, and improving the welfare of the people. Cao Cao emphasized the importance of maintaining a well-disciplined military and implemented a centralized bureaucratic system to streamline governance and enhance efficiency.

7. Literary Pursuits and Cultural Patronage

In addition to his military and political pursuits, Cao Cao was also a patron of the arts and an accomplished poet. He actively promoted literature, patronized scholars, and established a thriving cultural scene in his capital. Cao Cao's literary works, including his poetry and historical writings, provided insights into his personality, worldview, and aspirations.

Conclusion

Cao Cao's rise from a military commander to an imperial advisor was a testament to his exceptional leadership skills, strategic vision, and political acumen. His military achievements, consolidation of power, and governance reforms laid the foundation for the Kingdom of Wei's stability and prosperity. Cao Cao's influence extended beyond the battlefield, as he actively shaped the cultural and literary landscape of his time. In the subsequent chapters, we will further explore Cao Cao's reign, his conflicts with other kingdoms, and his enduring legacy in the Three Kingdoms period.

The Battle of Guandu: Cao Cao's Consolidation of Power

The Battle of Guandu, fought in 200 CE, was a pivotal moment in the rise of Cao Cao and the establishment of the Kingdom of Wei. This battle between Cao Cao and his rival warlord Yuan Shao marked a critical turning point in the power dynamics of the Three Kingdoms era. In this chapter, we will delve into the circumstances leading up to the Battle of Guandu, the strategic maneuvers employed by Cao Cao, the decisive moments of the battle, and its implications for Cao Cao's consolidation of power.

1. The Rivalry between Cao Cao and Yuan Shao

Cao Cao and Yuan Shao emerged as two prominent warlords vying for control over the central plains of China. Their rivalry stemmed from conflicting ambitions, competing claims to authority, and differences in political ideologies. Both leaders amassed considerable military forces and sought to establish their dominance over the region. The tension between Cao Cao and Yuan Shao set the stage for the fateful clash at Guandu.

2. Strategic Calculations and Preparations

Recognizing the need to secure his position and weaken his rival, Cao Cao carefully planned his campaign against Yuan Shao. He assessed the terrain, gathered intelligence, and strategically positioned his forces. Cao Cao understood the importance of resource management, logistics, and troop morale in determining the outcome of the battle. His preparations laid the groundwork for a meticulously planned offensive.

3. The Riverine Defense: Cao Cao's Strategic Advantage

One of Cao Cao's key advantages was his understanding of the region's geography and the strategic use of the Yellow River as a natural defense. By fortifying the riverbanks and controlling river crossings, Cao Cao effectively limited the mobility and options of Yuan Shao's forces. This defensive position gave Cao Cao a significant edge, forcing Yuan Shao to adapt to a challenging battlefield.

4. Yuan Shao's Strategic Errors

Yuan Shao, though initially commanding a larger army, made crucial strategic errors that played to Cao Cao's advantage. His lack of decisive action, internal divisions among his advisors, and logistical challenges weakened his position. Yuan Shao's failure to effectively coordinate his forces and exploit Cao Cao's vulnerabilities ultimately contributed to his defeat at Guandu.

5. The Decisive Battle

The Battle of Guandu began with a series of skirmishes and minor engagements as both sides tested each other's defenses. However, the decisive moment came when Cao Cao launched a surprise attack on Yuan Shao's main camp, exploiting a gap in his opponent's defenses. This bold maneuver caught Yuan Shao off guard and sent his forces into disarray. Cao Cao's well-disciplined troops and superior strategic command secured a resounding victory.

6. Implications and Aftermath

The Battle of Guandu had profound implications for the balance of power in the region. Cao Cao's victory not only solidified his control over the central plains but also dealt a severe blow to Yuan Shao's ambitions. The battle demonstrated Cao Cao's military genius, his ability to adapt to changing circumstances, and his strategic acumen. It elevated his reputation as a formidable warlord and cemented his position as a major player in the Three Kingdoms era.

7. Consolidation of Power and Political Influence

Following his victory at Guandu, Cao Cao used his military successes to consolidate his power and expand his influence. He garnered support from local elites, integrated defeated armies into his own forces, and implemented policies to win the loyalty of the people. Cao Cao's effective governance, administrative reforms, and patronage of talented individuals further strengthened his position as a leader.

Conclusion

The Battle of Guandu was a crucial chapter in Cao Cao's rise to power and his consolidation of the Kingdom of Wei. This decisive victory over Yuan Shao established Cao Cao as the dominant force in the central plains and paved the way for his future military campaigns and political ambitions. The battle showcased Cao Cao's strategic brilliance, resourcefulness, and leadership, setting the stage for the subsequent conflicts and power struggles of the Three Kingdoms era.

The Xuchang Administration: Establishing Wei's Capital

After consolidating his power and securing his position as a dominant force in the central plains, Cao Cao turned his attention to establishing a stable administrative center for the Kingdom of Wei. This chapter explores the founding of the Xuchang Administration, the capital of Wei, and the policies and reforms implemented by Cao Cao to govern his realm effectively. We will delve into the reasons for selecting Xuchang as the capital, the structure of the administration, the governance reforms, and the impact of Cao Cao's rule on the development of Wei.

1. Selecting Xuchang: Strategic Considerations

The choice of Xuchang as the capital of Wei was influenced by several strategic considerations. Situated in the heartland of the central plains, Xuchang provided a centralized location that allowed for efficient governance and easy access to various regions under Wei's control. Its proximity to the Yellow River facilitated transportation and trade, further enhancing its appeal as a capital city. Cao Cao recognized the advantages of Xuchang's geographic position and decided to establish his administration there.

2. Administrative Structure and Bureaucratic Reforms

Cao Cao implemented a well-organized administrative structure to govern the Kingdom of Wei. He established various departments and bureaus responsible for different aspects of governance, such as finance, agriculture, justice, and military affairs. The administration operated under a hierarchical system, with Cao Cao at the pinnacle of power, assisted by trusted advisors and officials. This bureaucratic system aimed to streamline governance, promote efficiency, and consolidate Cao Cao's authority.

3. Agrarian Reforms and Economic Development

Recognizing the importance of agriculture in sustaining the kingdom's prosperity, Cao Cao implemented agrarian reforms aimed at increasing agricultural productivity and improving the welfare of the farming population. He introduced policies to encourage land reclamation, improve irrigation systems, and promote efficient farming techniques. Cao Cao's focus on agricultural development laid the foundation for economic stability and ensured a steady food supply for the growing population.

4. Infrastructure Development and Urban Planning

Cao Cao invested in infrastructure development to support the growth of Xuchang as a bustling capital city. He initiated projects to expand and improve transportation networks, construct public buildings, and enhance the city's overall infrastructure. These efforts not only facilitated trade and commerce but also improved the living conditions of the city's inhabitants. Cao Cao's urban planning and development initiatives transformed Xuchang into a thriving center of economic and cultural activities.

5. Legal Reforms and Judicial System

Cao Cao recognized the importance of a fair and efficient legal system for maintaining social order and resolving disputes. He implemented legal reforms that aimed to standardize laws, ensure impartiality in judicial proceedings, and promote the rule of law. Cao Cao appointed competent judges and legal experts to uphold justice and enforce the law. These reforms fostered a sense of security and stability within Wei's territories.

6. Educational and Cultural Patronage

Cao Cao also emphasized the importance of education and culture in the development of Wei. He patronized scholars, established schools, and encouraged intellectual pursuits. Cao Cao's support for education and cultural activities not only attracted talented individuals to his administration but also fostered a vibrant intellectual environment in Xuchang.

7. Legacy and Impact

The establishment of the Xuchang Administration under Cao Cao's leadership had a lasting impact on the development of the Kingdom of Wei. His governance reforms, administrative structure, and emphasis on infrastructure and economic development laid the groundwork for Wei's stability and prosperity. The legacy of Cao Cao's rule in Xuchang continued to shape the subsequent reigns of his successors and influenced the course of the Three Kingdoms period.

Conclusion

The establishment of the Xuchang Administration marked a significant milestone in Cao Cao's reign and the governance of the Kingdom of Wei. Through strategic planning, administrative reforms, and infrastructure development, Cao Cao created a stable and prosperous capital city that became the center of political, economic, and cultural activities in Wei. The Xuchang Administration set a precedent for effective governance and laid the foundation for Wei's continued growth and influence in the Three Kingdoms era.

Cao Cao's Pursuit of the Emperor: A Bid for Legitimacy

Cao Cao, the influential warlord and ruler of the Kingdom of Wei, sought not only to consolidate his power but also to establish his legitimacy as a rightful leader. One of the significant aspects of his quest for legitimacy was his pursuit of Emperor Xian, the nominal ruler of the Han Dynasty. In this chapter, we will explore Cao Cao's motivations for pursuing the emperor, the strategies employed to gain his favor, the challenges he faced, and the implications of this bid for legitimacy.

1. Motivations and Rationale

Cao Cao's pursuit of Emperor Xian was driven by multiple factors. Firstly, he recognized the symbolic power of having the emperor under his control, which would grant him legitimacy and bolster his authority in the eyes of the people. Secondly, Cao Cao sought to use the emperor's position to strengthen his claim as the rightful successor to the Han Dynasty and to present himself as a unifying force. Lastly, by positioning himself as the protector of the emperor, Cao Cao aimed to win the support of those who remained loyal to the Han Dynasty.

2. Manipulating the Imperial Court

To secure Emperor Xian's cooperation, Cao Cao employed various strategies within the imperial court. He cultivated relationships with influential court officials, gained their trust, and gradually consolidated his influence over the court's decision-making processes. Cao Cao skillfully maneuvered political factions and used a combination of rewards, punishments, and political alliances to strengthen his position and weaken his rivals. Through these tactics, Cao Cao aimed to create a favorable environment for his bid to control the emperor.

3. The Emperor's Reluctant Alliance

Emperor Xian initially resisted Cao Cao's overtures, mindful of his symbolic role as the ruler of the Han Dynasty. However, faced with political pressure and the realities of the fractured empire, the emperor eventually acquiesced to Cao Cao's influence. He saw the warlord as a stabilizing force and accepted his protection, effectively becoming a figurehead under Cao Cao's control. This reluctant alliance provided Cao Cao with a semblance of legitimacy and further solidified his rule.

4. Challenges and Opposition

Cao Cao's pursuit of the emperor was not without challenges. He faced opposition from factions within his own camp who questioned the legitimacy of his actions and feared the concentration of power in his hands. Additionally, rival warlords and factions loyal to the Han Dynasty saw Cao Cao's control over the emperor as a threat to their own ambitions. Cao Cao had to navigate these challenges, maintaining a delicate balance of power while preserving the facade of Han Dynasty legitimacy.

5. Implications for Legitimacy and Authority

Cao Cao's successful bid for the emperor's cooperation significantly enhanced his legitimacy and authority. With Emperor Xian under his control, Cao Cao projected an image of being the de facto ruler, while still paying lip service to the Han Dynasty. He used the emperor's presence to consolidate his power, rally support from those who valued the imperial institution, and project an image of stability and continuity.

6. Opposition and Criticism

However, Cao Cao's pursuit of the emperor also attracted criticism and opposition. Some viewed his actions as a betrayal of the Han Dynasty and questioned his motives and loyalty. Others accused him of manipulating the emperor for his personal gain, undermining the authority of the imperial institution. These criticisms and perceptions shaped the narrative surrounding Cao Cao's rule and influenced the perception of his legitimacy in the eyes of later historians.

7. Legacy and Historical Assessment

Cao Cao's pursuit of Emperor Xian left a lasting impact on the Three Kingdoms period. His actions set a precedent for subsequent warlords to control the emperor, further eroding the authority of the Han Dynasty. The complex dynamics between Cao Cao and Emperor Xian shaped the political landscape and influenced the power struggles of the era. Historically, Cao Cao's pursuit of the emperor is seen as a strategic move to consolidate power, but it also generated debates about the legitimacy of his rule.

Conclusion

Cao Cao's pursuit of Emperor Xian was a pivotal aspect of his bid for legitimacy as the ruler of the Kingdom of Wei. Through political maneuvering, alliances, and careful manipulation of the imperial court, Cao Cao secured the emperor's cooperation, enhancing his authority and projecting an image of stability and continuity. However, his actions also attracted criticism and opposition, raising questions about the legitimacy of his rule and the role of the Han Dynasty. The pursuit of the emperor shaped the political landscape of the Three Kingdoms period and left a lasting impact on the historical narrative.

Chapter 3: Liu Bei and the Kingdom of Shu

The Virtuous Rebel: Liu Bei's Early Life and Ambitions

Liu Bei, a central figure in the Three Kingdoms period, was known for his charismatic leadership, unwavering determination, and embodiment of Confucian virtues. In this chapter, we delve into Liu Bei's early life, exploring his upbringing, personal experiences, and ambitions that set the stage for his rise as a virtuous rebel.

1. Origins and Family Background

To understand Liu Bei's character and motivations, it is crucial to examine his family background. Liu Bei hailed from a humble background, born into the Liu clan, a respected but financially modest family. He traced his lineage back to Emperor Jing of the Western Han Dynasty, which provided him with a sense of noble heritage. Despite his family's diminished social status, Liu Bei held on to the values and ideals associated with his ancestry, which would shape his actions later in life.

2. Early Life and Struggles

Liu Bei's early life was marked by hardships and challenges. After the early demise of his parents, he faced financial constraints and lived in relative obscurity. He took various odd jobs and traveled through different regions, seeking opportunities to make a living. These formative experiences not only instilled resilience and adaptability but also exposed Liu Bei to the diverse realities and needs of the common people, fostering a deep empathy that would become a defining characteristic of his leadership.

3. Embracing Confucian Virtues

Liu Bei's encounter with the teachings of Confucianism significantly influenced his worldview and shaped his aspirations. He embraced the Confucian virtues of benevolence, righteousness, loyalty, and filial piety, seeing them as guiding principles for a just and harmonious society. Liu Bei sought to embody these virtues in his actions and governance, positioning himself as a leader dedicated to serving the people and restoring the Han Dynasty's ideals.

4. Ambitions and the Pursuit of Power

Driven by his sense of righteousness and desire to restore order, Liu Bei harbored ambitions to play a significant role in the empire's affairs. He viewed himself as a guardian of the Han Dynasty and envisioned a future where he could establish a just and virtuous kingdom. Liu Bei's ambitions were not merely personal; they were deeply rooted in his belief that he had a moral obligation to restore peace and bring stability to the war-torn land.

5. Building Alliances and Brotherhood

Liu Bei's journey toward power was accompanied by the forging of crucial alliances and the establishment of brotherhood bonds. Notably, his deep friendship with Guan Yu and Zhang Fei, formed during his time in the Peach Garden Oath, became the foundation of his support network. These loyal and capable companions shared Liu Bei's vision and stood by his side throughout the tumultuous Three Kingdoms era, contributing to his eventual rise as a force to be reckoned with.

6. The Romance of the Three Kingdoms and Liu Bei's Image

The literary masterpiece "Romance of the Three Kingdoms" played a significant role in shaping Liu Bei's image and popular perception. The novel portrayed Liu Bei as the epitome of virtue, a charismatic leader whose actions exemplified benevolence, righteousness, and humility. While the novel is a work of fiction, it greatly influenced the way Liu Bei is remembered and admired, perpetuating the idealized image of the virtuous rebel.

7. Historical Assessment and Legacy

Despite the embellishments and idealization, Liu Bei's impact on the Three Kingdoms period cannot be denied. His commitment to Confucian values, his efforts to establish a just and virtuous kingdom, and his ability to inspire loyalty among his followers set him apart as a remarkable figure. Liu Bei's legacy extends beyond his own time, as his virtuous image and leadership style continue to resonate in Chinese culture and serve as a symbol of righteous governance.

Conclusion

Liu Bei's early life experiences, his embrace of Confucian virtues, and his unwavering determination to restore order and righteousness shaped his path as a virtuous rebel. His journey from humble beginnings to becoming a central figure in the Three Kingdoms period exemplifies the power of personal convictions and the impact of charismatic leadership. Liu Bei's story serves as an inspiration, representing the ideals of benevolence, righteousness, and loyalty that continue to captivate audiences and influence perceptions of leadership in the Three Kingdoms era.

The Oath of the Peach Garden: The Birth of Brotherhood

In the annals of Chinese history, few bonds are as celebrated as the brotherhood between Liu Bei, Guan Yu, and Zhang Fei. The Oath of the Peach Garden, a legendary event that took place during the Three Kingdoms period, solidified their loyalty and set the stage for their remarkable collaboration. In this chapter, we delve into the significance of the oath, its historical context, and the enduring impact it had on the Kingdom of Shu.

1. Historical Background: An Era of Turmoil

Before exploring the specifics of the Peach Garden oath, it is crucial to understand the historical context in which it occurred. The Three Kingdoms period was marked by political instability, wars, and power struggles. The collapse of the Han Dynasty had fragmented China into three distinct kingdoms: Wei, Shu, and Wu. Against this backdrop of chaos and uncertainty, Liu Bei, Guan Yu, and Zhang Fei's brotherhood emerged as a beacon of loyalty, trust, and unity.

2. Liu Bei, Guan Yu, and Zhang Fei: Origins and Personalities

To fully appreciate the significance of the oath, it is important to examine the backgrounds and personalities of the three individuals involved. Liu Bei, a virtuous and charismatic leader, embodied the ideals of benevolence and righteousness. Guan Yu, renowned for his unwavering loyalty and martial prowess, commanded respect and admiration. Zhang Fei, known for his fierce temperament and formidable strength, added a dynamic element to the trio. Together, they formed a powerful bond of brotherhood that would shape their destinies.

3. The Gathering at the Peach Garden

The Peach Garden oath is believed to have taken place in the spring of 191 CE. According to historical accounts, Liu Bei, Guan Yu, and Zhang Fei, recognizing their shared goals and values, swore a solemn oath under a peach tree. They pledged to support and protect one another, to fight for justice, and to work together to restore the Han Dynasty's glory. This sacred oath solidified their bond and set the foundation for their future endeavors.

4. Brotherhood in Action: Loyalty and Sacrifice

The oath of the Peach Garden was more than a symbolic gesture. It laid the groundwork for the unwavering loyalty and sacrifice displayed by Liu Bei, Guan Yu, and Zhang Fei throughout their lives. They remained fiercely devoted to one another, facing numerous challenges and hardships together. Their unwavering commitment to the oath and each other served as a source of strength and inspiration, forging a brotherhood that withstood the tests of time.

5. The Oath's Political and Strategic Implications

The Peach Garden oath had significant political and strategic implications. By solidifying their brotherhood, Liu Bei, Guan Yu, and Zhang Fei formed a powerful alliance that bolstered their collective strength. This alliance not only ensured mutual support in times of conflict but also served as a rallying point for those disillusioned by the chaos of the era. Their united front provided a sense of stability and legitimacy, attracting loyal followers and building a foundation for the Kingdom of Shu.

6. Literary Depictions and Popular Perceptions

The oath of the Peach Garden gained further prominence through its depiction in the literary masterpiece, "Romance of the Three Kingdoms." This novel, a fictionalized account of the Three Kingdoms era, heightened the mythical aura surrounding the oath and cemented its place in popular culture. The portrayal of the brotherhood as an unwavering bond of loyalty and righteousness captivated readers and elevated Liu Bei, Guan Yu, and Zhang Fei to legendary status.

7. Legacy and Influence

The Peach Garden oath's legacy extends far beyond the Three Kingdoms period. It has become an enduring symbol of loyalty, friendship, and devotion in Chinese culture. The story of Liu Bei, Guan Yu, and Zhang Fei continues to inspire and resonate with audiences, emphasizing the power of unity and the importance of shared values in times of adversity. The oath's influence can be seen in various aspects of Chinese society, from literature and art to business and interpersonal relationships.

Conclusion

The Oath of the Peach Garden stands as a testament to the unbreakable bond forged between Liu Bei, Guan Yu, and Zhang Fei. Their commitment to one another, as exemplified by this legendary oath, laid the foundation for their remarkable achievements and the establishment of the Kingdom of Shu. The Peach Garden oath serves as a timeless reminder of the enduring power of loyalty, trust, and brotherhood in the face of adversity, leaving a lasting legacy in Chinese history and culture.

The Battle of Red Cliffs: Liu Bei's Alliance Against Cao Cao

The Battle of Red Cliffs is one of the most pivotal events in the Three Kingdoms period. It marked a turning point in the struggle for dominance between the warlords Cao Cao and Liu Bei. This chapter delves into the historical significance, key players, strategic maneuvers, and the ultimate outcome of the Battle of Red Cliffs, highlighting its impact on the Kingdom of Shu.

1. Historical Context: Cao Cao's Ambitions and Liu Bei's Response

Before exploring the Battle of Red Cliffs, it is important to understand the political landscape of the time. Cao Cao, a powerful warlord, sought to unify China under his rule, while Liu Bei aimed to restore the Han Dynasty and bring peace and stability to the land. Their conflicting ambitions set the stage for a confrontation that would shape the course of history.

2. The Alliance of Liu Bei and Sun Quan

Recognizing the threat posed by Cao Cao, Liu Bei forged a crucial alliance with Sun Quan, the ruler of the Kingdom of Wu. This alliance brought together two formidable forces, uniting Liu Bei's military prowess and righteous cause with Sun Quan's naval strength and strategic resources. Their collaboration was instrumental in countering Cao Cao's advances and laying the foundation for the Battle of Red Cliffs.

3. Strategic Maneuvers and Preparations

As Cao Cao's forces advanced southward, Liu Bei and Sun Quan prepared to face the imminent threat. They strategically selected the Red Cliffs as the battleground, capitalizing on the geographical advantages of the Yangtze River and employing various tactics to overcome Cao Cao's superior numbers. The preparations, both on land and water, were crucial in setting the stage for the decisive battle that would follow.

4. Key Figures in the Battle

The Battle of Red Cliffs brought together renowned figures whose actions would shape the outcome of the conflict. Liu Bei, Sun Quan, and their respective generals, such as Zhuge Liang and Zhou Yu, played instrumental roles in devising strategies, rallying troops, and leading the charge against Cao Cao. These brilliant military minds and charismatic leaders left an indelible mark on the battle and the subsequent course of the Three Kingdoms period.

5. The Battle Unfolds: Naval Warfare and Fire Attack

The Battle of Red Cliffs unfolded in two key phases: naval warfare and a decisive fire attack. Sun Quan's navy, under the strategic guidance of Zhou Yu, engaged Cao Cao's forces in a fierce naval battle. The use of fire as a tactical weapon, famously employed by Zhuge Liang, turned the tide in favor of the allied forces. This crucial turning point showcased the brilliance of their military strategies and the effectiveness of their united front.

6. Aftermath and Historical Impact

The Battle of Red Cliffs resulted in a resounding victory for Liu Bei and Sun Quan, dealing a significant blow to Cao Cao's ambitions of unification. It not only preserved the independence of the southern warlords but also served as a catalyst for the subsequent power struggles and realignments in the Three Kingdoms period. The battle's outcome highlighted the importance of strategic planning, unity, and adaptability in the face of a formidable adversary.

7. Literary Depictions and Cultural Significance

The Battle of Red Cliffs has captured the imagination of generations through its depiction in the classic novel, "Romance of the Three Kingdoms." This masterpiece immortalized the key events and characters of the battle, further amplifying its historical significance and cultural impact. The battle's representation in literature, art, and popular culture continues to resonate with audiences, reinforcing its status as a legendary event in Chinese history.

Conclusion

The Battle of Red Cliffs stands as a testament to the power of strategic alliances, brilliant military tactics, and the determination of those who sought to resist Cao Cao's dominance. Liu Bei's alliance with Sun Quan, the strategic maneuvers employed, and the eventual victory at Red Cliffs played a pivotal role in shaping the Kingdom of Shu and influencing the course of the Three Kingdoms period. The battle's historical significance and cultural impact endure to this day, making it a defining moment in the narrative of the Three Kingdoms era.

The Establishment of Shu: Liu Bei's Quest for a Just Kingdom

The establishment of the Kingdom of Shu under the leadership of Liu Bei is a significant chapter in the Three Kingdoms period. This section explores Liu Bei's vision for a just and benevolent kingdom, his efforts to build a strong foundation, and the challenges he faced in realizing his aspirations.

1. Liu Bei's Ideals and Early Ambitions

To understand the establishment of Shu, it is essential to delve into Liu Bei's ideals and early ambitions. Liu Bei, known for his sense of righteousness and commitment to the principles of Confucianism, aimed to restore the glory of the Han Dynasty and bring peace and stability to the war-torn land. His vision for a just kingdom based on benevolence and virtue became the driving force behind his actions.

2. Gathering Support and Building Alliances

Liu Bei recognized that realizing his vision required building a strong network of support and alliances. He strategically formed relationships with influential figures such as Zhuge Liang, Pang Tong, and Liu Zhang, gaining their loyalty and assistance in his quest for power. These alliances played a crucial role in strengthening Liu Bei's position and establishing the foundation for the future Kingdom of Shu.

3. The Jing Province and the Battle of Yi Ling

One of the significant turning points in Liu Bei's quest for a just kingdom was the acquisition of the Jing Province. Through a series of strategic maneuvers and alliances, Liu Bei successfully seized control of the Jing Province, a critical region with strategic importance. The Battle of Yi Ling, a decisive conflict against the forces of Liu Zhang, solidified Liu Bei's control over the province and further advanced his goal of establishing Shu.

4. The Governance and Administration of Shu

With the acquisition of the Jing Province, Liu Bei faced the task of establishing a stable and just governance system. He sought the guidance of talented advisors, such as Zhuge Liang, to formulate policies that promoted social welfare, agricultural development, and fair governance. The administration of Shu under Liu Bei's leadership aimed to prioritize the well-being of the people and create a harmonious society.

5. Challenges and Setbacks

The establishment of Shu was not without challenges and setbacks. Liu Bei faced opposition from rival warlords, including Cao Cao and Sun Quan, who sought to undermine his authority and territorial ambitions. Internal conflicts and power struggles within Shu also posed significant obstacles to the realization of Liu Bei's vision. These challenges tested Liu Bei's leadership and required him to navigate complex political dynamics to maintain stability and advance his cause.

6. Legacy and Influence of Liu Bei's Shu

The establishment of Shu under Liu Bei's leadership left a lasting legacy in the history of China. Despite its eventual downfall, Shu's emphasis on benevolent governance, loyalty, and righteousness resonated with subsequent generations. The story of Liu Bei and the Kingdom of Shu became a symbol of virtue, inspiring future leaders and influencing the moral fabric of Chinese society.

7. Assessing Liu Bei's Quest for a Just Kingdom

This section critically evaluates Liu Bei's quest for a just kingdom and the achievements and shortcomings of his rule. It explores the impact of his governance philosophy, his leadership style, and the overall legacy of Shu. The assessment provides a balanced perspective on the extent to which Liu Bei succeeded in realizing his vision and the enduring significance of his ideals in Chinese history.

Conclusion

The establishment of the Kingdom of Shu under Liu Bei's leadership exemplified his unwavering commitment to creating a just and benevolent kingdom. Despite the challenges and setbacks, Liu Bei's vision and determination laid the foundation for a realm that prioritized virtue, loyalty, and the welfare of its people. The story of Shu stands as a testament to the enduring appeal of Liu Bei's ideals and his profound impact on the narrative of the Three Kingdoms period.

Chapter 4: Sun Quan and the Kingdom of Wu

Rise of the Sun Family: Sun Jian to Sun Quan

The rise of the Sun family and the establishment of the Kingdom of Wu played a crucial role in the Three Kingdoms period. This section explores the journey of Sun Jian, the founding of the Sun family's influence, and the subsequent rise to power of Sun Quan, culminating in the establishment of the Kingdom of Wu.

1. Sun Jian: The Patriarch of the Sun Family

To understand the rise of the Sun family, it is important to begin with Sun Jian, the patriarch and a prominent figure during the late Eastern Han Dynasty. Sun Jian was known for his military prowess, bravery, and loyalty. This section delves into his early life, military campaigns, and his contributions to the Han Dynasty.

2. Sun Ce: The Heir and Expansionist

Sun Jian's legacy was carried on by his son, Sun Ce, who continued the family's rise to power. This subsection explores Sun Ce's charismatic leadership, his military achievements, and his expansionist policies. Sun Ce's conquests and alliances laid the groundwork for the future Kingdom of Wu.

3. The Battle of Red Cliffs: Sun Quan's Ascendancy

The Battle of Red Cliffs was a turning point for the Sun family and the rise of Sun Quan. This subsection examines Sun Quan's role in the battle, his strategic alliances with Liu Bei, and the subsequent rise of the Kingdom of Wu. The significance of the battle in establishing Sun Quan's authority and expanding Wu's influence is explored in detail.

4. The Administration and Governance of Wu

With the establishment of the Kingdom of Wu, Sun Quan faced the task of governance and administration. This subsection delves into Sun Quan's policies, his efforts to consolidate power, and the establishment of a stable administration. It explores the key figures within Wu's government and their contributions to the kingdom's growth and stability.

5. Wu's Diplomatic Maneuvers and Expansion

The Kingdom of Wu was known for its diplomatic prowess and strategic alliances. This subsection explores Wu's diplomatic maneuvers, including its relationships with Shu and Wei, and its expansionist policies. Sun Quan's skillful diplomacy and military campaigns expanded Wu's territory and solidified its position as a major power in the Three Kingdoms period.

6. The Art of War: Sun Tzu's Influence

The Sun family's rise to power and the establishment of Wu were influenced by the teachings of Sun Tzu, a renowned military strategist. This subsection explores Sun Tzu's influence on Sun Jian, Sun Ce, and Sun Quan, and how his strategies shaped Wu's military tactics and decision-making.

7. Legacy and Impact of the Kingdom of Wu

The legacy of the Kingdom of Wu extends beyond its existence during the Three Kingdoms period. This subsection examines Wu's cultural contributions, its influence on subsequent dynasties, and its lasting impact on Chinese history and literature.

Conclusion

The rise of the Sun family, from Sun Jian to Sun Quan, and the establishment of the Kingdom of Wu mark a significant chapter in the Three Kingdoms period. Their military achievements, diplomatic maneuvers, and administrative prowess solidified Wu's position as one of the three major powers. The legacy of the Sun family and the Kingdom of Wu continue to be celebrated in Chinese history and culture, highlighting their enduring significance in shaping the narrative of the Three Kingdoms era.

The Battle of Chibi: Wu's Defining Victory over Cao Cao

The Battle of Chibi, also known as the Battle of Red Cliffs, is one of the most significant and iconic events in the Three Kingdoms period. This section explores the circumstances leading up to the battle, the strategic decisions made by Sun Quan and his allies, and the dramatic outcome that solidified Wu's position as a major power in the Three Kingdoms era.

1. Prelude to Conflict: Cao Cao's Southern Campaign

To understand the significance of the Battle of Chibi, it is important to examine the events leading up to it. This subsection explores Cao Cao's ambitious Southern Campaign, his motivations, and the military preparations he undertook to consolidate his power in the south. It also delves into the state of the various factions and their alliances prior to the battle.

2. Sun Quan's Alliance with Liu Bei

Recognizing the threat posed by Cao Cao's forces, Sun Quan forged a crucial alliance with Liu Bei, the ruler of Shu. This subsection delves into the diplomatic negotiations between Sun Quan and Liu Bei, their shared interests and objectives, and the formation of a united front against Cao

Cao. The strategic significance of this alliance in the context of the Battle of Chibi is explored.

3. The Strategic Importance of the Yangtze River

The Yangtze River played a pivotal role in the Battle of Chibi. This subsection examines the geographical significance of the river, the challenges and advantages it presented to both sides, and how it influenced the course of the battle. The utilization of naval tactics and the control of waterways become crucial elements in the conflict.

4. The Fire Attack: Zhou Yu's Ingenious Strategy

One of the most famous episodes of the Battle of Chibi is the fire attack orchestrated by Zhou Yu, the military strategist of Wu. This subsection delves into the planning and execution of this ingenious strategy, its impact on Cao Cao's forces, and the decisive turning point it created in the battle. The tactical brilliance of Zhou Yu and the bravery of Wu's warriors are highlighted.

5. The Naval Battle: Sun Quan's Triumph

While the fire attack is often emphasized, the naval battle that preceded it was also a significant aspect of the Battle of Chibi. This subsection explores the naval engagements between Wu and Wei, the tactics employed by both sides, and the leadership of Sun Quan in securing a decisive victory. The challenges faced by Wu's navy and their ultimate triumph are examined in detail.

6. Aftermath and Impact

The aftermath of the Battle of Chibi had far-reaching consequences for all three kingdoms. This subsection discusses the immediate effects of the battle on the balance of power, the morale of the forces involved, and the subsequent military campaigns and diplomatic developments. It also examines the long-term impact of the battle on the narrative of the Three Kingdoms period and its enduring significance in Chinese history and culture.

7. The Battle of Chibi in Literature and Popular Culture

The Battle of Chibi has captured the imagination of storytellers and artists throughout history. This subsection explores the portrayal of the battle in the famous novel "Romance of the Three Kingdoms," as well as its depiction in other forms of literature, art, and popular culture. The enduring legacy of the Battle of Chibi as a symbol of courage, strategy, and triumph is examined.

Conclusion

The Battle of Chibi stands as a defining moment in the history of the Three Kingdoms period. Wu's victory over Cao Cao not only ensured its survival but also established it as a major power in the region. The strategic decisions, tactical brilliance, and sheer determination displayed by Sun Quan and his allies during this battle have left an indelible mark on Chinese history and continue to captivate audiences around the world. The Battle of Chibi represents the resilience and resourcefulness of the Kingdom of Wu, exemplifying the complex and dramatic nature of the Three Kingdoms era.

Establishing the Kingdom of Wu: Sun Quan's Consolidation of Power

Introduction: The establishment of the Kingdom of Wu marks a crucial turning point in the Three Kingdoms period. This section explores the rise of Sun Quan and his efforts to solidify his authority, establish a stable governance structure, and expand Wu's influence in the region. Sun Quan's political acumen, military campaigns, and administrative reforms are examined in detail.

1. The Succession of Sun Quan: This subsection delves into the succession of Sun Quan as the leader of the Wu faction following the death of his father, Sun Jian. It explores the challenges he faced as a young ruler and how he navigated the complex web of political alliances and rivalries to consolidate his position. The support of key figures within the Wu faction and his own leadership qualities are highlighted.

2. Administrative Reforms: To establish a stable and efficient administration, Sun Quan implemented various reforms in the newly formed Kingdom of Wu. This subsection discusses his efforts to establish a bureaucratic system, promote meritocracy, and improve governance and taxation. The establishment of key government institutions

and the appointment of capable officials are examined, showcasing Sun Quan's commitment to effective governance.

3. Military Expansion and Diplomacy: Sun Quan recognized the importance of military strength and strategic alliances in securing Wu's position in the Three Kingdoms period. This subsection explores Sun Quan's military campaigns and alliances, both offensive and defensive, aimed at expanding Wu's territory and countering the influence of Wei and Shu. The battles and negotiations that shaped Wu's military and diplomatic strategies are analyzed.

4. Cultural and Economic Development: Sun Quan also focused on fostering cultural and economic development within the Kingdom of Wu. This subsection discusses his patronage of the arts, support for scholars, and promotion of cultural activities that contributed to Wu's intellectual and cultural vibrancy. Additionally, the economic policies implemented by Sun Quan to stimulate trade, agriculture, and infrastructure development are explored.

5. Relations with Shu and Wei: The complex relationships between the three kingdoms had a significant impact on the political landscape of the Three Kingdoms period. This subsection delves into Sun Quan's interactions with the Kingdom of Shu and the Kingdom of Wei, examining his shifting alliances, diplomatic negotiations,

and military engagements. The challenges and opportunities presented by these relationships are analyzed.

6. Challenges and Threats: Despite his successes, Sun Quan faced numerous challenges and threats to the stability of the Kingdom of Wu. This subsection explores the internal and external pressures that Sun Quan had to navigate, including rebellions, power struggles, and external invasions. The strategies employed by Sun Quan to overcome these challenges and maintain the integrity of Wu are examined.

7. Legacy and Historical Evaluation: This subsection assesses Sun Quan's legacy and his contributions to the Kingdom of Wu and the Three Kingdoms era as a whole. The historical evaluation of Sun Quan's reign, his leadership style, and the impact of his policies on Wu's longevity and influence are discussed. The enduring significance of the Kingdom of Wu in Chinese history and culture is also examined.

Conclusion: Sun Quan's establishment of the Kingdom of Wu marked a pivotal moment in the Three Kingdoms period. Through his political acumen, military prowess, and administrative reforms, Sun Quan successfully consolidated his power, expanded Wu's territory, and ensured its survival amidst the turbulent times. The Kingdom of Wu would go on to play a significant role in the ultimate fate of the Three Kingdoms, leaving a lasting impact on Chinese history.

The Southern Campaigns: Wu's Expansion and Diplomatic Maneuvers

Introduction: The Kingdom of Wu, led by Sun Quan, emerged as a formidable force during the Three Kingdoms period. This section explores Wu's ambitious southern campaigns and its diplomatic maneuvers to solidify its power and expand its territory. Sun Quan's military strategies, alliances, and conquests in the southern regions of China are examined in detail.

1. The Strategic Importance of Southern Regions: This subsection sets the stage by highlighting the strategic importance of the southern regions in the Three Kingdoms period. It discusses the geographical advantages, rich resources, and potential threats posed by the southern territories. The significance of Wu's expansion into these regions for its economic growth, military defense, and overall influence is emphasized.

2. Wu's Southern Conquests: Sun Quan recognized the need to secure Wu's control over the southern territories to strengthen his kingdom. This subsection delves into Wu's military campaigns in the south, including the conquest of territories such as Jing Province, Changsha, and Hefei. The key battles, strategies, and challenges faced by Wu's forces

are analyzed, showcasing the military prowess of Sun Quan's armies.

3. Diplomatic Maneuvers: In addition to military conquests, Sun Quan skillfully employed diplomacy to expand Wu's influence in the southern regions. This subsection explores the diplomatic alliances and negotiations undertaken by Sun Quan to secure the loyalty of local rulers and tribes. The establishment of vassal states and the integration of local power structures into Wu's governance are examined.

4. Naval Supremacy: The southern campaigns highlighted the naval prowess of the Kingdom of Wu. This subsection discusses Wu's development of a formidable navy, its naval tactics, and its dominance in naval warfare. The construction of naval fleets, the training of marines, and the utilization of river networks for strategic advantage are explored, showcasing Wu's naval supremacy.

5. The Subjugation of Nanman: Wu's southern campaigns also involved subjugating the Nanman tribes, who occupied the rugged and untamed regions of southern China. This subsection delves into the challenges faced by Wu's forces in dealing with the fierce resistance of the Nanman tribes. The military strategies employed to pacify

and assimilate these tribal groups into Wu's dominion are examined.

6. Consolidation of Power and Governance: As Wu expanded its territory in the south, it faced the challenge of consolidating power and establishing effective governance structures. This subsection explores the administrative reforms implemented by Sun Quan to ensure the smooth integration of the newly acquired territories. The appointment of local officials, taxation policies, and the promotion of cultural assimilation are discussed.

7. Cultural and Economic Impact: Wu's expansion into the southern regions had significant cultural and economic implications. This subsection examines the cultural exchanges between Wu and the southern territories, including the spread of Wu's customs, language, and governance systems. The economic development resulting from Wu's control over fertile agricultural lands, trade routes, and natural resources is also explored.

8. Relations with Wei and Shu: The southern campaigns had implications not only for Wu's internal development but also for its relationships with the Kingdom of Wei and the Kingdom of Shu. This subsection analyzes Wu's diplomatic interactions, military alliances, and conflicts with its neighboring kingdoms. The complex dynamics and

shifting alliances that characterized Wu's relations with Wei and Shu are examined.

Conclusion: Wu's southern campaigns under the leadership of Sun Quan played a crucial role in shaping the Kingdom of Wu and its prominence during the Three Kingdoms period. Through strategic military conquests, diplomatic maneuvers, and effective governance, Wu expanded its territory, secured its borders, and established a strong presence in the southern regions of China. The cultural, economic, and political impact of Wu's expansion is evident in its lasting influence on the history of the Three Kingdoms era.

Chapter 5: Alliances and Betrayals

The Shu-Wu Alliance: Liu Bei and Sun Quan's Unsteady Partnership

Introduction: The alliances and betrayals that unfolded during the Three Kingdoms period played a significant role in shaping the course of history. This section focuses on the complex and often tumultuous partnership between Liu Bei of Shu and Sun Quan of Wu. The establishment, challenges, and ultimate fate of the Shu-Wu alliance are explored, shedding light on the intricate dynamics of power, trust, and ambition in this era.

1. Historical Background: To understand the context of the Shu-Wu alliance, this subsection provides a historical background on the relationship between Liu Bei and Sun Quan. It delves into their individual ambitions, the initial encounters between their respective kingdoms, and the factors that led to their eventual alliance.

2. The Formation of the Shu-Wu Alliance: This subsection examines the circumstances that led Liu Bei and Sun Quan to form the alliance. It explores the political, military, and strategic considerations that prompted their decision to join forces against their common enemy, Cao Cao of Wei. The negotiation process, the terms of the alliance, and the shared goals of Shu and Wu are analyzed.

3. The Battle of Chibi: A Test of Alliance: The Battle of Chibi, one of the most famous battles in Chinese history, serves as a critical turning point in the Shu-Wu alliance. This subsection provides an in-depth analysis of the battle, highlighting the crucial role played by both Liu Bei and Sun Quan in the decisive victory over Cao Cao's forces. The strategies employed, the coordination between Shu and Wu armies, and the impact of the victory on the alliance are examined.

4. Challenges and Strains: While the Battle of Chibi solidified the initial success of the Shu-Wu alliance, it also marked the beginning of challenges and strains in their partnership. This subsection explores the factors that led to conflicts and mistrust between Liu Bei and Sun Quan. The competing interests, conflicting ambitions, and disagreements over territorial claims are discussed, highlighting the fragility of their alliance.

5. Betrayals and Broken Promises: As the alliance faced increasing pressures, betrayals and broken promises began to emerge. This subsection delves into the instances of betrayal and treachery that occurred within the Shu-Wu alliance. The actions of key individuals, such as Guan Yu and Lu Meng, and their impact on the alliance are examined. The

consequences of these betrayals and the subsequent fallout between Shu and Wu are explored.

6. Diplomatic Efforts and Reconciliation: Despite the challenges, both Liu Bei and Sun Quan recognized the importance of maintaining the alliance against the common threat of Wei. This subsection discusses the diplomatic efforts made by Shu and Wu to mend their relationship and reconcile their differences. The role of intermediaries, peace treaties, and diplomatic gestures in restoring the alliance are analyzed.

7. Shifting Loyalties and Alliances: The Shu-Wu alliance was not the only alliance in the Three Kingdoms period, and the shifting loyalties of other factions had a significant impact on its stability. This subsection explores the influence of other kingdoms, warlords, and individuals on the Shu-Wu alliance. The complexities of forming and maintaining alliances amidst a backdrop of changing loyalties and shifting power dynamics are examined.

8. The End of the Shu-Wu Alliance: Despite attempts at reconciliation, the Shu-Wu alliance eventually met its demise. This subsection delves into the events and factors that led to the dissolution of the alliance. The final conflicts, betrayals, and the ultimate severing of ties between Shu and

Wu are explored, shedding light on the consequences of their fractured partnership.

Conclusion: The Shu-Wu alliance stands as a testament to the intricate nature of alliances and the challenges faced by leaders during the Three Kingdoms period. The unsteady partnership between Liu Bei and Sun Quan exemplifies the complexities of balancing personal ambitions, territorial disputes, and the need for unity against a common enemy. The legacy of the Shu-Wu alliance and its impact on the broader narrative of the Three Kingdoms era are reflected upon, offering insights into the nature of alliances and betrayals in historical and political contexts.

The Battle of Yiling: Liu Bei's Confrontation with Wu

Introduction: In the turbulent era of the Three Kingdoms, alliances were formed and shattered, and betrayals were a constant threat. This section focuses on the significant confrontation between Liu Bei, the ruler of Shu, and Sun Quan, the leader of Wu, known as the Battle of Yiling. This battle was a pivotal moment in the Shu-Wu alliance and had far-reaching consequences for the balance of power in the Three Kingdoms. In this subsection, we will explore the events leading up to the Battle of Yiling, analyze the strategies employed by both sides, and examine the outcome and aftermath of this critical clash.

1. The Context of Tension: To understand the build-up to the Battle of Yiling, this subsection provides the historical context and underlying tensions between Liu Bei and Sun Quan. It delves into the territorial disputes, conflicting ambitions, and growing mistrust that strained their fragile alliance. The political maneuvers and diplomatic efforts leading to the escalation of hostilities are examined.

2. Preparations and Strategies: As tensions mounted, both Liu Bei and Sun Quan began preparing for the inevitable clash. This subsection explores the military preparations, strategic considerations, and alliances forged

in anticipation of the Battle of Yiling. The deployment of troops, fortifications, and the gathering of resources by both sides are examined, shedding light on their respective strategies and the significance of the impending confrontation.

3. The Battle Unfolds: The Battle of Yiling was a protracted conflict that tested the strength and resolve of both Shu and Wu. This subsection provides a detailed account of the battle, from the initial skirmishes to the decisive engagements that shaped its outcome. The strategies, tactics, and key military leaders on both sides are analyzed, painting a vivid picture of the fierce and chaotic nature of the battle.

4. The Role of Liu Bei: As the ruler of Shu, Liu Bei's leadership and decisions were instrumental in the Battle of Yiling. This subsection explores Liu Bei's strategic choices, command decisions, and personal involvement in the battle. His motivations, battlefield prowess, and the impact of his actions on the outcome of the conflict are examined, offering insights into his role as a military leader.

5. The Role of Sun Quan: Sun Quan, as the leader of Wu, played a crucial role in the Battle of Yiling. This subsection delves into Sun Quan's strategies, tactical maneuvers, and leadership during the conflict. The alliances

he forged, his engagement with key military commanders, and the impact of his decisions on the outcome of the battle are analyzed, highlighting his role as a formidable adversary.

6. Turning Points and Critical Engagements: Within the larger battle, there were critical turning points and engagements that shaped its course. This subsection examines the key moments, decisive encounters, and critical factors that influenced the outcome of the Battle of Yiling. The impact of terrain, weather, surprise maneuvers, and the performance of specific units or commanders are analyzed, providing a nuanced understanding of the battle's ebb and flow.

7. Outcome and Aftermath: The Battle of Yiling had significant repercussions for both Shu and Wu. This subsection explores the outcome of the battle and its aftermath. The territorial changes, political consequences, and the long-term effects on the Shu-Wu alliance are examined. The impact of the battle on Liu Bei's ambitions, Sun Quan's hold on power, and the broader dynamics of the Three Kingdoms are discussed.

8. Historical Perspectives and Legacy: The Battle of Yiling holds a prominent place in the history of the Three Kingdoms era. This subsection discusses the historical perspectives on the battle and its significance. The views of

contemporary and later historians, as well as the portrayal of the battle in literary works, such as the "Romance of the Three Kingdoms," are explored. The enduring legacy of the Battle of Yiling and its impact on subsequent events in the Three Kingdoms period are also examined.

Conclusion: The Battle of Yiling serves as a microcosm of the alliances and betrayals that defined the Three Kingdoms era. It showcased the fierce competition for power, the complexities of military strategy, and the personal ambitions of the key leaders involved. The Battle of Yiling had far-reaching consequences, altering the balance of power between Shu and Wu and reshaping the course of the Three Kingdoms. Its exploration offers valuable insights into the nature of conflict, alliances, and the complexities of navigating the intricate political landscape of the time.

The Battle of Xiaoting: Shu and Wu's Final Clash

Introduction: Within the tumultuous Three Kingdoms era, alliances were forged and broken, leading to significant battles that shaped the fate of the kingdoms. One such battle was the Battle of Xiaoting, the final clash between the kingdoms of Shu and Wu. This subsection explores the events leading up to the battle, the strategies employed by both sides, the unfolding of the conflict itself, and the far-reaching consequences it had on the Three Kingdoms. Through an in-depth analysis of the Battle of Xiaoting, we gain insights into the intricate dynamics of alliances and betrayals during this transformative period.

1. Setting the Stage: To understand the significance of the Battle of Xiaoting, it is essential to delve into the context and background that led to the conflict. This subsection provides an overview of the strained Shu-Wu alliance, the growing tensions between Liu Bei and Sun Quan, and the political landscape that precipitated the final clash. The territorial disputes, conflicting ambitions, and key figures involved are examined.

2. Preparations and Strategies: Both Shu and Wu recognized the stakes involved in the Battle of Xiaoting and undertook extensive preparations and strategic considerations. This subsection delves into the military

preparations, alliances sought, and the strategic planning undertaken by Liu Bei and Sun Quan. The deployment of troops, fortifications, and the gathering of resources are explored, shedding light on the strategies employed by both sides.

3. The Battlefield: The Battle of Xiaoting took place in a strategic location, and the geography played a crucial role in shaping the tactics and outcomes of the conflict. This subsection provides an in-depth analysis of the battlefield, including its topography, natural features, and tactical advantages and disadvantages for both Shu and Wu. The impact of the terrain on the battle's dynamics is examined.

4. Shu's Offensive: Liu Bei, the ruler of Shu, launched a major offensive against Wu, aiming to consolidate his power and expand his territory. This subsection explores Shu's offensive strategies, the key objectives set by Liu Bei, and the military tactics employed by Shu's generals. The roles of key figures such as Zhuge Liang and Zhao Yun are highlighted, providing insights into their contributions to the Shu offensive.

5. Wu's Defense: As Shu pressed forward, Wu, under the leadership of Sun Quan, mounted a robust defense to protect its territory and maintain its position. This subsection examines Wu's defensive strategies, the

fortifications erected, and the military maneuvers employed by Wu's generals. The roles of key figures such as Lu Xun and Gan Ning are explored, shedding light on their efforts to repel Shu's advances.

6. The Clash of Armies: The Battle of Xiaoting was marked by intense and protracted clashes between the armies of Shu and Wu. This subsection provides a detailed account of the battles and skirmishes that took place, highlighting key engagements, troop movements, and the strategies employed by both sides. The ebb and flow of the battle, pivotal moments, and the performance of notable commanders are analyzed.

7. Outcome and Aftermath: The Battle of Xiaoting had significant ramifications for both Shu and Wu. This subsection examines the outcome of the battle and its aftermath, including the territorial changes, casualties, and the impact on the balance of power between the two kingdoms. The political and military consequences for Liu Bei, Sun Quan, and their respective kingdoms are discussed, offering insights into the far-reaching implications of the battle.

8. Historical Perspectives and Legacy: The Battle of Xiaoting holds a prominent place in the history of the Three Kingdoms era. This subsection explores the perspectives of

historians and scholars on the battle, examining their assessments of the strategies employed, the key players involved, and the overall significance of the clash. Furthermore, the enduring legacy of the Battle of Xiaoting and its impact on subsequent events and historical narratives are discussed.

Conclusion: The Battle of Xiaoting marked the final clash between the kingdoms of Shu and Wu, bringing an end to their uneasy alliance and setting the stage for further political shifts in the Three Kingdoms era. This critical battle exemplified the complex dynamics of alliances and betrayals that characterized the period, showcasing the strategies, military prowess, and personal ambitions of Liu Bei, Sun Quan, and their generals. The Battle of Xiaoting serves as a testament to the intricacies of power struggles and the decisive role of military engagements in shaping the destiny of the Three Kingdoms.

Shifting Loyalties: Generals and Advisors Amidst Turmoil

Introduction: The Three Kingdoms period was characterized by intricate webs of alliances, betrayals, and shifting loyalties among the warlords, generals, and advisors. This subsection delves into the complex landscape of allegiances during this turbulent era. Focusing on the key figures who played pivotal roles in shaping the alliances and betrayals, we examine their motivations, the factors that influenced their decisions, and the consequences of their actions. By exploring the narratives of these generals and advisors, we gain insights into the intricate dynamics of power, loyalty, and personal ambition that unfolded amidst the chaos of the Three Kingdoms.

1. The Importance of Loyalty: Before delving into the shifting loyalties, it is essential to establish the significance of loyalty in the context of the Three Kingdoms. This subsection explores the concept of loyalty in Chinese culture, its deep-rooted historical context, and its centrality in the relationships between rulers and their subordinates. The expectations, obligations, and conflicts associated with loyalty are examined, providing a foundation for understanding the motivations and dilemmas faced by the generals and advisors.

2. The Influential Figures: This section introduces the key generals and advisors who played instrumental roles in the alliances and betrayals during the Three Kingdoms era. Figures such as Guan Yu, Zhang Fei, Zhuge Liang, Sima Yi, Zhou Yu, and Jia Xu are among those explored in depth. Their backgrounds, capabilities, and personal ambitions are examined, shedding light on the factors that influenced their loyalty and the subsequent shifts in their allegiances.

3. The Early Alliances: This subsection delves into the initial alliances formed among the warlords and their generals during the early stages of the Three Kingdoms era. The alliances between Liu Bei, Guan Yu, and Zhang Fei, known as the Oath of the Peach Garden, are explored, along with their early collaborations and the bonds forged through mutual trust and shared aspirations. The initial allegiances and their impact on subsequent events are analyzed.

4. The Fragmentation of Loyalties: As the Three Kingdoms era progressed, the landscape of alliances became increasingly fragmented, leading to a series of shifting loyalties among the generals and advisors. This subsection examines the factors that contributed to the fragmentation of loyalties, such as territorial disputes, conflicting ambitions, personal rivalries, and changing political dynamics. The internal struggles within factions, the influence of external

forces, and the complexities of navigating allegiances in a turbulent era are explored.

5. Betrayals and Consequences: Betrayals were a recurring theme in the Three Kingdoms era, with generals and advisors frequently switching sides to pursue personal gain or survival. This subsection delves into notable instances of betrayals, such as Guan Yu's defection to Cao Cao, and their far-reaching consequences on the alliances and the overall course of the war. The motivations behind these betrayals, be it ambition, strategic considerations, or personal grievances, are examined, highlighting the profound impact they had on the balance of power.

6. Loyalty and Strategy: The relationship between loyalty and strategic considerations is a complex one in the Three Kingdoms era. This subsection explores the strategic calculations made by the generals and advisors, weighing loyalty to their lord against the prospects of success and survival. The strategic implications of loyalty shifts, the tactical advantages gained, and the challenges faced in managing shifting alliances are analyzed, providing insights into the delicate balance between loyalty and self-interest.

7. Legacy and Interpretations: The shifting loyalties among the generals and advisors during the Three Kingdoms era continue to capture the imagination of historians,

scholars, and storytellers. This subsection examines the diverse interpretations and evaluations of these figures, their loyalties, and their actions. The enduring legacy of these individuals, both in historical records and in popular culture, is explored, shedding light on the ever-evolving narratives surrounding their motivations and the moral dilemmas they faced.

Conclusion: The complex landscape of shifting loyalties among the generals and advisors during the Three Kingdoms era reflects the multifaceted nature of power, ambition, and survival in a time of turmoil. By delving into the motivations, actions, and consequences of these key figures, we gain a deeper understanding of the intricate dynamics that shaped the alliances and betrayals. The exploration of shifting loyalties offers valuable insights into the complexities of human nature and the challenges faced by those seeking to navigate the treacherous political landscape of the Three Kingdoms.

Chapter 6: The Final Struggle for Supremacy

Sima Yi's Rise to Power: From Wei Strategist to Regent

Introduction: The Three Kingdoms period reached its climax in a fierce struggle for supremacy among the kingdoms of Wei, Shu, and Wu. In this chapter, we delve into the rise of Sima Yi, a brilliant strategist and statesman who played a pivotal role in the final stages of the conflict. From his early career as a military officer to his ascension as the de facto ruler of Wei, we explore Sima Yi's rise to power, his strategic brilliance, and the impact of his actions on the course of the Three Kingdoms.

1. Early Life and Military Career: To understand Sima Yi's rise to power, it is crucial to examine his early life and military career. This section provides an overview of Sima Yi's background, including his family lineage and his early experiences in military service. We explore his early achievements, his reputation as a capable officer, and the skills and qualities that set him apart from his peers.

2. Service under Cao Cao: Sima Yi's association with the ruling Cao clan proved instrumental in his rise to prominence. This subsection focuses on Sima Yi's service under Cao Cao, the influential warlord who founded the Wei Kingdom. We examine Sima Yi's contributions to Cao Cao's

military campaigns, his strategic acumen, and his ability to navigate the complex political landscape of Wei. Additionally, we explore the trust and respect Cao Cao had for Sima Yi, which laid the foundation for his future rise to power.

3. The Battle of Red Cliffs and Its Aftermath: The Battle of Red Cliffs was a critical turning point in the Three Kingdoms period. This subsection explores Sima Yi's involvement in this pivotal battle, his assessment of the situation, and his strategic recommendations to Cao Cao. We analyze the aftermath of the battle, including the defeat of Cao Cao's forces and the subsequent challenges faced by Wei. Sima Yi's role in salvaging Wei's position and regaining Cao Cao's trust is examined, showcasing his strategic foresight and resilience.

4. Consolidating Power in Wei: After the Battle of Red Cliffs, Sima Yi continued to rise in prominence within the Wei Kingdom. This section explores Sima Yi's efforts to consolidate his power and influence within the Wei court. We examine his political maneuvering, alliances, and patronage networks that allowed him to solidify his position as a trusted advisor to the Wei rulers. Sima Yi's administrative reforms, military strategies, and diplomatic

endeavors are analyzed, highlighting his abilities as a capable statesman.

5. The Regency and Sima Yi's Influence: As the Wei Kingdom faced internal power struggles and external threats, Sima Yi's influence grew even further. This subsection focuses on Sima Yi's assumption of regency over Wei, effectively becoming the de facto ruler. We explore the challenges he faced in maintaining control, his efforts to centralize power, and his policies to stabilize the kingdom. Sima Yi's strategic vision, governance style, and ability to balance the interests of different factions are examined, showcasing his effectiveness as a leader.

6. Confrontation with Shu and Wu: Sima Yi's rise to power coincided with increased tensions between Wei, Shu, and Wu. This section delves into Sima Yi's confrontations with the other two kingdoms, particularly his strategic encounters with the Kingdom of Shu, led by Liu Bei's successor, Liu Shan. We examine Sima Yi's military campaigns, his strategies to counter Shu's advances, and the challenges he faced in maintaining Wei's dominance in the conflict.

7. Legacy and Historical Perspectives: The legacy of Sima Yi is analyzed in this subsection, exploring how his rise to power and his actions shaped the trajectory of the Three

Kingdoms period. We assess the impact of his governance, military strategies, and political reforms on the Wei Kingdom and the broader historical narrative. Furthermore, we delve into the various historical perspectives and evaluations of Sima Yi, including both praise and criticism, shedding light on the complex and often contradictory portrayals of this influential figure.

Conclusion: Sima Yi's rise to power from a capable strategist to the de facto ruler of Wei exemplifies the fluid and dynamic nature of the Three Kingdoms period. His strategic brilliance, political maneuvering, and leadership abilities played a pivotal role in shaping the final stages of the conflict. Sima Yi's legacy as a statesman and strategist continues to be a subject of fascination and debate among historians and scholars, showcasing the enduring significance of his contributions to the Three Kingdoms era.

The Battle of Hefei: Wei's Defense against Shu's Northern Campaigns

Introduction: As the Three Kingdoms period neared its climax, the struggle for supremacy intensified among the Kingdoms of Wei, Shu, and Wu. In this chapter, we explore the pivotal Battle of Hefei, a significant conflict that took place between the Kingdom of Wei and the Kingdom of Shu. This subtopic focuses on the battle's context, key figures involved, strategic maneuvers, and its impact on the overall balance of power. Through a detailed analysis of the Battle of Hefei, we gain insights into the military strategies and challenges faced by both sides in their quest for dominance.

1. Background and Context: To understand the significance of the Battle of Hefei, it is essential to delve into the background and context that led to the conflict. This section provides an overview of the strategic situation in the Three Kingdoms during this period, including the power dynamics between Wei and Shu. We examine Shu's northern campaigns, its motivations for expansion, and the strategic objectives behind targeting Hefei, a key stronghold of Wei.

2. Key Figures and Leadership: The Battle of Hefei witnessed the involvement of prominent military leaders and strategists from both Wei and Shu. This subsection highlights the key figures and their roles in the conflict. We

explore the strategies and decision-making of Wei's commanders, such as Zhang Liao and Yue Jin, known for their tactical prowess and defensive capabilities. Additionally, we delve into the leadership of Shu's generals, including Zhao Yun and Zhang Fei, who played crucial roles in the northern campaigns.

3. The Opening Moves: This section provides an analysis of the opening moves of the Battle of Hefei. We examine the strategies employed by both sides, including Shu's initial assaults and Wei's defensive measures. The geographical advantages and challenges of the Hefei region are explored, shedding light on the tactical considerations and obstacles faced by the armies.

4. Wei's Defensive Tactics: One of the defining aspects of the Battle of Hefei was Wei's defensive tactics. This subsection delves into the strategies employed by Wei to repel Shu's advances. We explore the construction of defensive fortifications, the deployment of troops, and the utilization of Wei's geographical advantages to create a formidable defense. The leadership and decision-making of Wei's commanders in the face of Shu's relentless assaults are analyzed, showcasing their ability to withstand and repel the enemy.

5. Shu's Offensive Strategies: Shu's northern campaigns and its approach to the Battle of Hefei were marked by bold and aggressive strategies. This section focuses on Shu's offensive maneuvers, including their attempts to breach Wei's defenses and capture Hefei. We analyze the tactics employed by Shu's commanders, their assessment of the battlefield, and their efforts to overcome Wei's defensive measures. The challenges faced by Shu's forces and their adaptability in the face of Wei's resolute defense are examined.

6. The Turning Point and Aftermath: Every battle has a turning point that shapes its outcome. In the Battle of Hefei, a significant event or strategic decision played a decisive role in determining the final outcome. This subsection explores the turning point of the battle and its ramifications for both Wei and Shu. We assess the impact of this event on the overall balance of power in the Three Kingdoms and the subsequent course of the conflict.

7. Historical Significance and Legacy: The Battle of Hefei holds historical significance as a pivotal engagement in the final struggle for supremacy during the Three Kingdoms period. This section delves into the long-term implications of the battle and its legacy. We examine how the battle influenced the strategies and alliances of the participating

Kingdoms, and its impact on the broader historical narrative. Furthermore, we discuss the differing historical perspectives and evaluations of the Battle of Hefei, shedding light on its enduring significance.

Conclusion: The Battle of Hefei stands as a testament to the military prowess, strategic thinking, and resilience displayed by both Wei and Shu during the Three Kingdoms era. Through a comprehensive analysis of this significant conflict, we gain insights into the challenges faced by the Kingdoms and the strategies employed to achieve their objectives. The Battle of Hefei played a crucial role in shaping the final struggle for supremacy, leaving a lasting impact on the historical legacy of the Three Kingdoms period.

The Ambitions of Jiang Wei: Shu's Last Stand

Introduction: In the closing chapters of the Three Kingdoms period, the Kingdom of Shu found itself in a precarious position, engaged in a desperate struggle for survival against the Kingdom of Wei. At the center of Shu's last stand was Jiang Wei, a talented and ambitious general who played a crucial role in the kingdom's military campaigns. This subtopic focuses on Jiang Wei's rise to prominence, his strategic initiatives, and the challenges he faced as he sought to uphold the fading hopes of Shu. Through a comprehensive exploration of Jiang Wei's ambitions, military campaigns, and their impact on Shu's fate, we gain valuable insights into the final stages of the Three Kingdoms period.

1. Early Life and Career of Jiang Wei: To understand the motivations and ambitions of Jiang Wei, it is essential to delve into his early life and career. This section provides an overview of Jiang Wei's background, including his upbringing, education, and early military experiences. We explore the formative influences that shaped his character, highlighting the key factors that contributed to his rise within the ranks of the Shu military.

2. Jiang Wei's Role in Shu's Military: Jiang Wei's ascent to power within the Kingdom of Shu was closely tied

to his military prowess and strategic acumen. This subsection focuses on Jiang Wei's role as a general in the Shu army and his contributions to the kingdom's military campaigns. We examine his tactical innovations, command style, and his ability to inspire and lead his troops. Furthermore, we explore his relationship with Liu Shan, the ruler of Shu, and the influence he wielded within the kingdom.

3. Jiang Wei's Ambitions and Vision: Jiang Wei's ambitions extended beyond mere military success; he had a vision for the future of Shu and its role in the Three Kingdoms. This section delves into the ambitions and aspirations of Jiang Wei, exploring his desire to expand Shu's territory, reclaim lost lands, and challenge the dominance of Wei. We analyze his strategic initiatives, including the Northern Expeditions, which aimed to establish Shu as the preeminent power in the Three Kingdoms.

4. Challenges and Setbacks: Despite his talents and aspirations, Jiang Wei faced numerous challenges and setbacks during his military campaigns. This subsection explores the difficulties he encountered, ranging from Wei's superior resources and defenses to internal issues within the Shu kingdom. We examine the strategic mistakes made by

Jiang Wei and their impact on Shu's fortunes, as well as the growing disillusionment within Shu's ranks due to the prolonged conflicts.

5. The Decline of Shu and Jiang Wei's Legacy: As Shu's fate hung in the balance, Jiang Wei's military endeavors ultimately proved insufficient to reverse the tide. This section examines the decline of Shu and the ultimate fall of the kingdom, despite Jiang Wei's efforts. We analyze the critical factors that led to Shu's demise, including the weakening internal situation, Wei's military countermeasures, and the shifting political landscape of the Three Kingdoms. Additionally, we evaluate Jiang Wei's legacy and his portrayal in historical accounts, highlighting the debates surrounding his role in Shu's downfall.

6. Historical Assessment and Interpretations: The actions and ambitions of Jiang Wei have been subject to differing interpretations among historians. This subsection explores the historical assessments of Jiang Wei's character, capabilities, and contributions to the Three Kingdoms narrative. We examine the varying viewpoints and evaluate the strengths and weaknesses of different perspectives, shedding light on the complex and multifaceted nature of Jiang Wei's historical legacy.

Conclusion: Jiang Wei's ambitions and military endeavors during the final stages of the Three Kingdoms period encapsulate the struggles, aspirations, and complexities of Shu's last stand. Through a comprehensive exploration of Jiang Wei's rise to prominence, his strategic initiatives, and the challenges he faced, we gain valuable insights into the dynamics of power, ambition, and the relentless pursuit of victory in the tumultuous era of the Three Kingdoms. Jiang Wei's legacy remains a subject of historical debate, underscoring the enduring fascination with the complex figures and events that shaped this pivotal period in Chinese history.

Wu's Surrender: The End of the Three Kingdoms War

Introduction: As the Three Kingdoms period drew to a close, the Kingdom of Wu found itself as one of the last contenders vying for supremacy. This subtopic focuses on Wu's surrender, marking the end of the Three Kingdoms War and the beginning of a new era in Chinese history. By examining the circumstances leading to Wu's decision to submit to the Kingdom of Wei, we gain insights into the political, military, and strategic considerations that shaped the final outcome of the conflict. This section delves into the events that led to Wu's surrender, the key players involved, and the consequences it had for the wider landscape of China.

1. The State of Wu at the Close of the Three Kingdoms Period: To understand the context in which Wu's surrender took place, it is important to examine the state of the kingdom at the time. This subsection provides an overview of Wu's military strength, its territorial holdings, and its relationship with the other kingdoms, particularly Wei and Shu. We explore the challenges faced by Wu, including internal strife, external pressures, and the shifting dynamics of the Three Kingdoms.

2. Sun Quan and the Decision to Surrender: Sun Quan, the ruler of Wu, played a pivotal role in the decision to surrender. This section explores the factors that influenced Sun Quan's choice, including the military stalemate, the exhaustion of resources, and the prospects of continued resistance. We delve into the internal debates within Wu's court, the advice of key advisors, and Sun Quan's own calculations and motivations. Additionally, we examine the negotiations with Wei and the terms of surrender.

3. The Fall of Wu's Mighty Generals: Wu was known for its formidable generals who had played significant roles throughout the Three Kingdoms period. This subsection focuses on the fate of Wu's renowned military leaders, such as Lu Xun, Gan Ning, and Lu Meng, in the face of the decision to surrender. We analyze their reactions, their responses to the changing political landscape, and the impact of Wu's surrender on their careers and legacies.

4. The Consequences of Wu's Surrender: Wu's surrender had far-reaching consequences for the political map of China and the subsequent dynastic transition. This section explores the aftermath of Wu's submission to Wei, including the consolidation of power by the Sima clan and the establishment of the Jin dynasty. We examine the fate of Wu's ruling family, the assimilation of Wu's territories into

the Wei domain, and the impact on the lives of Wu's subjects.

5. Historical Assessment and Interpretations: The surrender of Wu and the subsequent end of the Three Kingdoms War have been subject to various interpretations among historians. This subsection explores the historical assessments of Wu's surrender, including debates over Sun Quan's decision, the military and political realities faced by Wu, and the significance of the event in Chinese history. We evaluate different viewpoints and discuss the enduring legacy of Wu and its surrender in shaping the narrative of the Three Kingdoms period.

6. The Legacy of the Three Kingdoms War: The surrender of Wu marked the end of a prolonged period of conflict and the beginning of a new era in Chinese history. This section reflects on the broader legacy of the Three Kingdoms War, examining its impact on the subsequent dynasties, the development of Chinese culture, and its enduring resonance in literature, art, and popular culture.

Conclusion: The surrender of Wu brought an end to the Three Kingdoms War, concluding an era of intense conflict and setting the stage for the rise of the Jin dynasty. Wu's decision to submit to Wei was influenced by a complex interplay of factors, including military realities, political calculations, and the aspirations of its rulers. By analyzing the surrender of Wu, we gain a deeper understanding of the final chapter of the Three Kingdoms period and its lasting impact on the course of Chinese history.

Chapter 7: Legacy and Aftermath

Assessing the Three Kingdoms: Historical Perspectives and Controversies

Introduction: The Three Kingdoms period stands as one of the most fascinating and influential periods in Chinese history. This subtopic delves into the complex task of assessing the Three Kingdoms, exploring the diverse historical perspectives and controversies surrounding this era. By examining different interpretations, evaluating key debates, and analyzing the lasting impact of the Three Kingdoms, we gain a deeper understanding of its significance and the multiple layers of its historical legacy.

1. The Formation of Historical Narratives: The study of the Three Kingdoms period has evolved over centuries, shaped by the perspectives and biases of different historians and scholars. This section examines the origins of historical narratives surrounding the Three Kingdoms, from early historical records to later interpretations in literature, drama, and popular culture. We explore how these narratives have shaped public perception and influenced scholarly analysis.

2. Historical Sources and Interpretations: One of the challenges in assessing the Three Kingdoms is the limited availability and reliability of historical sources. This

subsection discusses the primary sources, including historical texts such as the Records of the Three Kingdoms, as well as archaeological discoveries and other forms of evidence. We explore the strengths and limitations of these sources and the interpretive choices made by historians in reconstructing the history of the period.

3. Key Debates and Controversies: The Three Kingdoms period has been the subject of lively debates among historians, each offering different perspectives on significant events, personalities, and their impact. This section highlights some of the key debates, such as the assessment of Cao Cao's legacy, the role of Liu Bei as a virtuous leader, and the military strategies employed by various factions. We delve into the contrasting viewpoints, examining the arguments, evidence, and theories put forth by different scholars.

4. Portrayals in Literature and Popular Culture: The Three Kingdoms period has captured the imagination of writers, playwrights, and artists throughout history. This subsection explores the enduring influence of literary works such as Romance of the Three Kingdoms and their impact on shaping popular perceptions of the era. We examine the depiction of key figures, the blending of history and fiction,

and the ways in which these portrayals have shaped our understanding of the Three Kingdoms.

5. Cultural and Social Legacy: Beyond its historical significance, the Three Kingdoms period has left a lasting impact on Chinese culture and society. This section explores the cultural legacy of the Three Kingdoms, including its influence on literature, art, philosophy, and political thought. We examine how the themes of loyalty, heroism, and stratagems continue to resonate in Chinese society and the ways in which the Three Kingdoms have been invoked as symbols in different historical periods.

6. Comparative Perspectives: To gain a broader understanding of the Three Kingdoms, it is valuable to consider comparative perspectives. This subsection explores connections and comparisons between the Three Kingdoms period and other historical periods or conflicts around the world. We examine parallels with ancient Rome, feudal Japan, or European medieval history, shedding light on universal themes of power, politics, and human ambition.

7. Relevance and Significance: This section reflects on the enduring relevance and significance of the Three Kingdoms period. We discuss its impact on Chinese historiography, its portrayal in contemporary media, and its lessons for governance, leadership, and strategy. We

examine how the study of the Three Kingdoms continues to contribute to our understanding of historical cycles, the complexities of human nature, and the dynamics of power.

Conclusion: The assessment of the Three Kingdoms is an ongoing endeavor that requires careful consideration of historical sources, diverse perspectives, and ongoing debates. By exploring the historical narratives, key controversies, and cultural legacy of the Three Kingdoms, we gain a deeper appreciation of this complex period and its enduring impact on Chinese history and beyond. The assessment of the Three Kingdoms invites us to reflect on the complexities of historical interpretation and the role of history in shaping our understanding of the past.

Literary Influence: "Romance of the Three Kingdoms" and Popular Perception

Introduction: Among the various literary works inspired by the Three Kingdoms period, "Romance of the Three Kingdoms" (Sanguo Yanyi) holds a prominent position. This subtopic delves into the enduring influence of "Romance of the Three Kingdoms" on popular perception of the era. We explore the origins and composition of the novel, its impact on Chinese literature and culture, and its role in shaping our understanding of the Three Kingdoms.

1. The Composition of "Romance of the Three Kingdoms": "Romance of the Three Kingdoms," written by Luo Guanzhong during the Ming Dynasty, is a monumental work of historical fiction. This section delves into the composition and structure of the novel, examining its narrative style, character development, and incorporation of historical events. We explore the sources and inspirations behind Luo Guanzhong's work and discuss the novel's significance as a literary masterpiece.

2. The Characters of "Romance of the Three Kingdoms": One of the key elements that contributed to the enduring popularity of "Romance of the Three Kingdoms" is its rich cast of characters. This subsection examines the portrayal of major figures such as Liu Bei, Cao Cao, and Sun

Quan, as well as lesser-known characters like Zhuge Liang and Lu Bu. We delve into their fictionalized representations, exploring how their traits, actions, and relationships have shaped popular perception and cultural imagination.

3. Blending History and Fiction: "Romance of the Three Kingdoms" artfully combines historical events with imaginative storytelling. This section explores the interplay between historical accuracy and fictional elements in the novel. We discuss the creative liberties taken by Luo Guanzhong, the incorporation of myths and legends, and the blending of historical facts with dramatic narratives. We examine how these literary devices have contributed to the enduring appeal and accessibility of the novel.

4. Popularization and Adaptations: "Romance of the Three Kingdoms" has achieved widespread popularity and has been adapted into various forms of media. This subsection explores the novel's journey from literary masterpiece to popular culture phenomenon. We discuss the impact of stage adaptations, television series, films, and video games that have brought the Three Kingdoms narrative to a broader audience. We examine the ways in which these adaptations have influenced popular perception and understanding of the era.

5. Cultural and Artistic Depictions: Beyond its influence on popular culture, "Romance of the Three Kingdoms" has also inspired various artistic forms, including traditional Chinese painting, calligraphy, and sculpture. This section explores the artistic representations of the Three Kingdoms, examining how visual artists have interpreted and depicted the novel's iconic scenes, characters, and themes. We discuss the role of art in reinforcing and reimagining popular perceptions of the Three Kingdoms.

6. Mythologizing and Symbolism: "Romance of the Three Kingdoms" has played a significant role in mythologizing the Three Kingdoms period. This subsection explores the creation of heroic myths, legendary battles, and iconic episodes that have become deeply ingrained in popular consciousness. We examine the symbolic meanings attributed to key figures and events in the novel, exploring how these symbols have been utilized in different historical periods to convey political messages or moral lessons.

7. Critiques and Reevaluations: While "Romance of the Three Kingdoms" has enjoyed immense popularity, it has also faced criticism for its romanticized and idealized portrayals. This section delves into scholarly critiques of the novel, examining the debates surrounding its historical accuracy, ideological biases, and literary merit. We discuss

how contemporary historians and scholars have reevaluated the novel's impact on the study of the Three Kingdoms period and its role in shaping historical narratives.

Conclusion: "Romance of the Three Kingdoms" has left an indelible mark on popular perception, cultural imagination, and scholarly discourse surrounding the Three Kingdoms era. Its powerful storytelling, memorable characters, and enduring themes continue to captivate audiences worldwide. By exploring the literary influence of "Romance of the Three Kingdoms" and its impact on popular perception, we gain insight into the dynamic relationship between history, literature, and collective memory.

Echoes of the Past: The Impact of the Three Kingdoms on Later Dynasties

Introduction: The Three Kingdoms period not only shaped the course of Chinese history but also left a profound impact on subsequent dynasties and the collective memory of the Chinese people. This subtopic explores the echoes of the Three Kingdoms in later dynasties, examining how rulers, scholars, and artists drew inspiration from this period. We delve into the enduring legacy of the Three Kingdoms and its influence on popular perception, literature, art, and political ideologies.

1. Historical Records and Imperial Legitimacy: The historical records of the Three Kingdoms, such as the "Records of the Three Kingdoms" (Sanguozhi), became invaluable sources for later dynasties. This section explores how rulers, particularly during the Tang, Song, and Ming dynasties, used the history of the Three Kingdoms to establish their own legitimacy. We examine how emperors sought to associate themselves with the virtuous rulers of the past and employed the Three Kingdoms narrative to reinforce their authority.

2. The Three Kingdoms in Neo-Confucian Thought: The philosophical and ethical teachings of Confucianism played a significant role in shaping Chinese society. This

subsection explores how Neo-Confucian scholars, such as Zhu Xi and Wang Yangming, drew upon the Three Kingdoms period to illustrate their moral and political theories. We discuss how concepts of loyalty, filial piety, and righteous governance were interpreted through the lens of the Three Kingdoms, influencing the intellectual discourse of later dynasties.

3. The Three Kingdoms in Literature and Drama: The Three Kingdoms period has been a constant source of inspiration for literary works and theatrical performances throughout Chinese history. This section explores the numerous novels, plays, and poems that continued the narrative of the Three Kingdoms or drew upon its themes and characters. We discuss famous works such as "Romance of the Three Kingdoms" and "The Peach Blossom Fan," examining how these literary creations contributed to the perpetuation of the Three Kingdoms legacy.

4. Visual Representations: Art and Iconography: The visual representations of the Three Kingdoms in paintings, sculptures, and other artistic mediums have left a lasting imprint on Chinese art history. This subsection explores how artists depicted the events and characters of the Three Kingdoms, examining the iconic imagery associated with the period. We discuss the use of symbolism, the portrayal of key

figures, and the artistic styles employed in capturing the essence of the Three Kingdoms.

5. Martial Arts and Popular Culture: The martial prowess and strategies displayed by the Three Kingdoms' heroes have had a profound impact on Chinese martial arts and popular culture. This section explores how martial arts schools and practitioners drew inspiration from the military strategies and combat techniques of the Three Kingdoms. We discuss the depiction of famous generals such as Guan Yu and Zhang Fei in martial arts fiction, films, and video games, examining their enduring popularity and influence.

6. Political Ideologies and Historical Analogies: The Three Kingdoms period has been frequently invoked throughout Chinese history as a historical analogy for political situations and power struggles. This subsection explores how political leaders, intellectuals, and revolutionaries utilized the Three Kingdoms narrative to express their political ideologies or criticize the ruling regime. We examine examples such as the Ming-Qing transition, the May Fourth Movement, and the Chinese Communist Revolution to illustrate the diverse ways in which the Three Kingdoms were invoked.

7. Regional Identity and Local Festivals: The Three Kingdoms narrative has also become intertwined with

regional identity and local festivals in certain parts of China. This section explores how provinces such as Sichuan, Hubei, and Jiangxi, which were significant locations during the Three Kingdoms period, have embraced the historical legacy through festivals, cultural events, and tourism. We discuss the cultural significance of these celebrations and their role in fostering a sense of local pride and historical continuity.

Conclusion: The echoes of the Three Kingdoms resonate across the tapestry of Chinese history, leaving an enduring impact on subsequent dynasties, literature, art, popular culture, and regional identity. The continuing fascination with the Three Kingdoms reflects its timeless appeal as a tale of heroism, political intrigue, and the complexities of human ambition. By examining the influence of the Three Kingdoms on later dynasties and popular perception, we gain insights into the enduring legacy of this pivotal era in Chinese history.

Lessons from the Three Kingdoms: Relevance in Modern Society

Introduction: The Three Kingdoms period, with its intricate web of alliances, betrayals, and power struggles, continues to captivate audiences even in modern times. This subtopic explores the lessons and values that can be gleaned from the Three Kingdoms narrative and its relevance in contemporary society. We delve into the enduring popularity of the Three Kingdoms, its portrayal in popular media, and the lessons it offers for leadership, strategy, and human nature.

1. Leadership and Governance: The Three Kingdoms period provides rich insights into the qualities of effective leadership and governance. This section examines the leadership styles and strategies employed by the key figures of the era, such as Liu Bei, Cao Cao, and Sun Quan. We explore themes of benevolence, righteousness, and strategic decision-making, and discuss their applicability in modern-day leadership contexts.

2. Strategy and Tactics: The military campaigns and strategic maneuvers in the Three Kingdoms period offer valuable lessons in warfare and strategy. This subsection delves into the art of war as depicted in the Three Kingdoms narrative, analyzing the tactics employed by military

commanders and the importance of adaptability, intelligence gathering, and resource management. We explore how these lessons can be applied in contemporary military and business contexts.

3. Ethics and Morality: The Three Kingdoms narrative raises ethical and moral dilemmas that continue to resonate with modern audiences. This section delves into the notions of loyalty, betrayal, righteousness, and personal integrity as portrayed in the Three Kingdoms. We examine the complex choices faced by characters such as Zhuge Liang, Guan Yu, and Lu Bu, and discuss their ethical implications in navigating contemporary moral challenges.

4. Human Nature and Psychology: The Three Kingdoms narrative offers profound insights into the depths of human nature and psychology. This subsection explores themes of ambition, greed, honor, and the complexities of human relationships. We analyze the psychological motivations and character traits of key figures in the Three Kingdoms, providing a nuanced understanding of human behavior and its relevance in modern society.

5. Lessons in Diplomacy and Alliances: The intricate web of alliances, negotiations, and diplomatic maneuvers in the Three Kingdoms period offers valuable lessons in the realm of diplomacy. This section explores the dynamics of

diplomacy and the challenges of forming and maintaining alliances amidst shifting loyalties and conflicting interests. We examine the strategies employed by Liu Bei, Sun Quan, and Cao Cao and their implications for contemporary diplomacy.

6. Resilience and Adaptability: The Three Kingdoms period was marked by constant change, uncertainty, and adversity. This subsection explores the resilience and adaptability displayed by the characters in the face of challenges and setbacks. We discuss how individuals and organizations can draw inspiration from the Three Kingdoms narrative to navigate modern-day complexities and embrace change with resilience.

7. Popular Perception and Media Influence: The popularity of the Three Kingdoms narrative has extended beyond historical accounts, permeating various forms of popular media. This section examines the portrayal of the Three Kingdoms in contemporary literature, films, television series, and video games. We discuss the impact of these portrayals on popular perception and the extent to which they accurately reflect the historical events and lessons of the Three Kingdoms.

Conclusion: The enduring popularity of the Three Kingdoms narrative is a testament to its timeless appeal and the lessons it offers for contemporary society. From leadership and strategy to ethics and diplomacy, the Three Kingdoms period continues to provide valuable insights into human nature and the complexities of navigating power dynamics. By analyzing the lessons from the Three Kingdoms and exploring their relevance in modern society, we can glean wisdom from the past and apply it to the challenges and opportunities of the present.

Conclusion

The Legacy of the Three Kingdoms: Reflections on a Transformative Era

Introduction: As we conclude our exploration of the Three Kingdoms period, it is essential to reflect on its enduring legacy and the impact it has had on historical understanding, cultural identity, and popular perception. This final subtopic delves into the lasting influence of the Three Kingdoms, both in academia and popular culture, and offers reflections on the significance of this transformative era.

1. Historical Legacy: The Three Kingdoms period holds a significant place in Chinese history, marking a critical transition from the Han Dynasty and paving the way for the subsequent dynasties. This section discusses the historical legacy of the Three Kingdoms, examining its impact on political structures, governance systems, and the evolution of military strategies. We explore the scholarly perspectives on the Three Kingdoms as a turning point in Chinese history and its lasting influence on subsequent dynasties.

2. Cultural Identity: The Three Kingdoms narrative has become deeply ingrained in Chinese cultural identity. This subsection explores how the stories and characters of

the Three Kingdoms have shaped Chinese literature, art, and popular culture. We examine the symbolism associated with key figures such as Liu Bei, Cao Cao, and Zhuge Liang, and their representation in traditional Chinese opera, literature, and visual arts. We also discuss the significance of the Three Kingdoms in fostering a sense of national pride and cultural heritage among the Chinese people.

3. Interpretations and Perspectives: The Three Kingdoms period has been subject to diverse interpretations and perspectives throughout history. This section analyzes different scholarly viewpoints on the Three Kingdoms, including traditional Chinese historical accounts, modern academic research, and alternative perspectives. We explore the debates surrounding key events, characters, and the overall narrative of the Three Kingdoms, highlighting the challenges of reconstructing history and the importance of critical analysis in understanding the era.

4. Popular Perception and Media Influence: The popularity of the Three Kingdoms extends far beyond historical research, permeating popular culture in various forms. This subsection delves into the impact of popular media adaptations, such as "Romance of the Three Kingdoms," films, television series, and video games, on the public's perception of the era. We examine how these

adaptations have shaped the collective imagination and influenced popular understanding of the Three Kingdoms. We also discuss the potential benefits and limitations of such popular media portrayals in conveying historical accuracy.

5. Lessons and Contemporary Relevance: The Three Kingdoms narrative offers valuable lessons and insights that continue to resonate in contemporary society. This section reflects on the enduring relevance of the Three Kingdoms era, exploring how the themes of leadership, strategy, ethics, and resilience can be applied to modern-day contexts. We discuss the ways in which individuals, organizations, and even nations can draw inspiration from the experiences and lessons of the Three Kingdoms to navigate complex challenges and foster positive change.

6. The Three Kingdoms in Global Perspective: While the Three Kingdoms period is deeply rooted in Chinese history, its influence has transcended national borders. This subsection examines the global impact of the Three Kingdoms narrative, particularly in East Asia and beyond. We explore its reception and adaptation in different cultures, its influence on literature and media outside of China, and its significance as a shared cultural reference point in East Asian societies. We also discuss the potential for cross-

cultural understanding and dialogue through the lens of the Three Kingdoms.

Conclusion: The Three Kingdoms period stands as a testament to the transformative power of history and its enduring impact on collective memory and popular perception. From its historical legacy and cultural significance to its portrayal in popular media, the Three Kingdoms continue to captivate and inspire people around the world. By reflecting on its legacy, interpreting its narratives, and drawing lessons from its complexities, we can gain a deeper understanding of this transformative era and its relevance in shaping our present and future.

Note: The content provided here is a suggested structure for the subtopic "The Legacy of the Three Kingdoms: Reflections on a Transformative Era" and Popular Perception." You may further expand on each section and include specific examples, arguments, and insights based on your research and knowledge of the topic.

The Three Kingdoms Unveiled: Inviting Readers to Explore Further

Introduction: As we reach the conclusion of our exploration into the fascinating world of the Three Kingdoms, it is important to acknowledge that our journey has only scratched the surface of this vast and complex historical period. This final subtopic, "The Three Kingdoms Unveiled: Inviting Readers to Explore Further and Popular Perception," aims to encourage readers to delve deeper into the subject matter, offering suggestions for further research, recommended readings, and considerations regarding the popular perception of the Three Kingdoms.

1. Exploring the Three Kingdoms: The Three Kingdoms period encompasses a rich tapestry of history, culture, and human drama. This section highlights the importance of continued exploration and research into this era, encouraging readers to engage with primary sources, academic works, and historical documents. It provides guidance on how to navigate the vast array of available resources, including books, scholarly articles, online platforms, and museum exhibitions, to deepen one's understanding of the Three Kingdoms.

2. Recommended Readings: To aid readers in their pursuit of knowledge about the Three Kingdoms, this

subsection presents a curated list of recommended readings. It includes both classic and contemporary works that offer unique perspectives on the era, its key figures, and significant events. The list encompasses academic studies, historical narratives, biographies, and fictional adaptations, providing a comprehensive selection for readers of different interests and backgrounds.

3. Online Resources and Digital Media: In today's digital age, online resources play a crucial role in accessing information and engaging with historical content. This section highlights reputable websites, databases, and online platforms that offer valuable resources on the Three Kingdoms. It also acknowledges the influence of digital media, such as podcasts, documentaries, and educational videos, in disseminating historical knowledge and promoting public engagement.

4. Interpreting Popular Perception: The popular perception of the Three Kingdoms has been shaped by various mediums, including literature, films, television series, and video games. This subsection encourages readers to critically analyze these portrayals and consider their impact on public understanding. It examines the balance between entertainment value and historical accuracy, urging readers to approach popular adaptations with a discerning

eye while appreciating their role in sparking interest and introducing the Three Kingdoms to wider audiences.

5. Engaging with the Three Kingdoms Community: The Three Kingdoms has garnered a dedicated community of enthusiasts, scholars, and fans who share a passion for this era. This section highlights the importance of engaging with this community through forums, discussion groups, conferences, and academic networks. It encourages readers to participate in conversations, exchange ideas, and contribute to the ongoing discourse surrounding the Three Kingdoms.

6. The Three Kingdoms' Enduring Relevance: The legacy of the Three Kingdoms extends far beyond its historical context. This subsection explores the enduring relevance of the era's themes, values, and lessons in contemporary society. It discusses how the principles of leadership, strategic thinking, loyalty, and moral governance espoused by the Three Kingdoms' figures can resonate with individuals, organizations, and even nations today. It prompts readers to reflect on the applicability of the Three Kingdoms' wisdom to their own lives and endeavors.

Conclusion: As we bring our exploration of the Three Kingdoms to a close, it becomes evident that the era's allure and impact are far-reaching. The invitation to explore further is extended to readers, encouraging them to continue their journey into the intricacies of the Three Kingdoms through continued research, engagement with recommended readings, and active participation in the Three Kingdoms community. By delving deeper into this transformative period, readers can gain a richer understanding of its historical significance, cultural influence, and enduring relevance in our world today.

Gratitude and Acknowledgments: Contributors to Unveiling the Past

Introduction: As we conclude our exploration of the Three Kingdoms, it is essential to express our gratitude and acknowledge the many contributors who have played a significant role in unveiling the past and shaping our understanding of this remarkable historical era. This final subtopic, "Gratitude and Acknowledgments: Contributors to Unveiling the Past and Popular Perception," aims to recognize the individuals, institutions, and scholars who have contributed to our knowledge of the Three Kingdoms. It also explores the impact of their work on popular perception and highlights the importance of continued research and collaboration.

1. Scholars and Historians: At the forefront of our gratitude are the scholars and historians who have dedicated their lives to the study of the Three Kingdoms. Their meticulous research, scholarly publications, and insightful analysis have shed light on the complexities of this period. This section acknowledges their contributions and highlights key figures who have significantly shaped our understanding of the Three Kingdoms through their groundbreaking research and influential works.

2. Archivists and Curators: Behind the scenes, archivists and curators play a vital role in preserving and making historical materials accessible to researchers and the general public. This subsection expresses gratitude to the individuals and institutions responsible for safeguarding and organizing historical documents, artifacts, and relics related to the Three Kingdoms. Their efforts in maintaining archives, museums, and libraries ensure that future generations can continue to explore and learn from the past.

3. Translators and Interpreters: The Three Kingdoms' rich literary and historical texts have been preserved through the work of translators and interpreters. This section acknowledges their contribution in bridging the linguistic and cultural gaps, enabling readers around the world to access and appreciate the primary sources and classic works related to the Three Kingdoms. Their dedication to accurate and nuanced translation helps to maintain the integrity of these texts and promotes a deeper understanding of the era.

4. Collaborative Research Projects: The study of the Three Kingdoms often involves collaboration among scholars, institutions, and research projects. This subsection highlights the importance of collaborative efforts in advancing our knowledge of the era. It recognizes the significance of interdisciplinary research, international

collaborations, and academic networks that foster dialogue, exchange of ideas, and shared resources. These collaborative endeavors contribute to a more comprehensive understanding of the Three Kingdoms and its historical significance.

5. Cultural Institutions and Media: Popular perception of the Three Kingdoms has been shaped by various cultural institutions and media platforms. This section acknowledges the contributions of filmmakers, television producers, authors, and video game developers who have brought the Three Kingdoms to life in popular culture. Their creative interpretations have introduced the era to wider audiences, sparking interest and curiosity. While artistic license may be employed, their works have played a role in popularizing the Three Kingdoms and inspiring further exploration.

6. Readers and Enthusiasts: Last but not least, this subsection expresses gratitude to the readers, enthusiasts, and fans of the Three Kingdoms who have shown a passionate interest in the era. Their curiosity, engagement, and continued support contribute to the vitality and ongoing study of the Three Kingdoms. Whether through academic pursuits, discussions, fan communities, or personal research,

their enthusiasm and dedication help to sustain interest and expand our collective knowledge.

Conclusion: In concluding our exploration of the Three Kingdoms, we extend our heartfelt gratitude and acknowledgments to the countless individuals and institutions who have contributed to our understanding of this transformative era. From scholars and historians to archivists, translators, and cultural creators, their collective efforts have unveiled the past and shaped popular perception. Their dedication, passion, and expertise have enriched our knowledge and appreciation of the Three Kingdoms.

As we move forward, it is crucial to recognize the ongoing importance of collaboration, interdisciplinary research, and the preservation of historical materials. The Three Kingdoms will continue to inspire and captivate generations to come, and it is through the collective efforts of scholars, cultural institutions, media platforms, and engaged readers that we can ensure its enduring legacy.

By expressing gratitude and acknowledging the contributions of these remarkable individuals and entities, we invite readers to join us in further exploring the rich tapestry of the Three Kingdoms. The journey does not end here but rather opens doors to new avenues of research, interpretation, and discovery. Let us continue to delve into the complexities of this era, fostering a deeper understanding of the past and its relevance to the present and future.

As we conclude our study, we express our sincere appreciation to all those who have played a role in unveiling the past, shaping our knowledge, and igniting our imagination. Together, let us carry the legacy of the Three Kingdoms forward, continuing to uncover its hidden treasures and sharing its timeless lessons with the world.

THE END

Wordbook

Welcome to the glossary section of this book. Here you will find a comprehensive list of key terms and their corresponding definitions related to the topics covered in the book. This section serves as a quick reference guide to help you better understand and navigate the content presented.

Key Terms and Definitions:

1. Three Kingdoms: Refers to the historical period in China from 220 to 280 AD, characterized by the division of the Han Dynasty into three major states: Wei, Shu, and Wu.

2. Eastern Han Dynasty: The ruling dynasty in China from 25 to 220 AD, preceding the Three Kingdoms period. It experienced significant political and social unrest, leading to its decline.

3. Decline of the Eastern Han Dynasty: Refers to the gradual weakening and eventual collapse of the Eastern Han Dynasty due to factors such as political corruption, peasant uprisings, and internal power struggles.

4. Rise of Three Kingdoms: The emergence of the Wei, Shu, and Wu states during the decline of the Eastern Han Dynasty, marking the fragmentation of China into three distinct political entities.

5. Warlords: Powerful military commanders who seized control of territories during the period of political

disintegration, often engaging in power struggles and territorial disputes.

6. Yellow Turban Rebellion: A significant uprising during the Eastern Han Dynasty, led by the Yellow Turban Sect, which protested against social and economic injustices, contributing to the overall decline of the dynasty.

7. Abdication of Emperor Xian: The voluntary relinquishment of the Han throne by Emperor Xian, marking the official split of the empire into the three kingdoms and the end of the Eastern Han Dynasty.

8. Cao Cao: A prominent warlord and political figure who rose to power during the Three Kingdoms period, eventually establishing the Kingdom of Wei.

9. Liu Bei: A key figure in the Three Kingdoms era, known for his role as the founder of the Kingdom of Shu and his pursuit of a just and righteous government.

10. Sun Quan: The founder and first emperor of the Kingdom of Wu, one of the three kingdoms during the Three Kingdoms period.

11. Battle of Red Cliffs: A pivotal battle fought between the allied forces of Liu Bei and Sun Quan against the army of Cao Cao, resulting in a decisive victory for the allied forces.

12. Sima Yi: A prominent strategist and general who played a crucial role in the Wei state during the Three

Kingdoms period, eventually becoming the de facto ruler as regent.

13. Shu-Wu Alliance: An alliance formed between Liu Bei's Kingdom of Shu and Sun Quan's Kingdom of Wu, marked by periods of cooperation, but also strained by conflicts and betrayals.

14. Battle of Yiling: A significant battle between the forces of Liu Bei's Shu and Sun Quan's Wu, resulting in a victory for Wu and further straining the Shu-Wu alliance.

15. Battle of Xiaoting: The final major clash between the forces of Shu and Wu, ultimately leading to the defeat of Shu and the consolidation of Wu's power.

16. Legacy of the Three Kingdoms: The enduring impact and influence of the Three Kingdoms period on Chinese history, culture, literature, and popular perception.

17. Romance of the Three Kingdoms: A renowned historical novel written by Luo Guanzhong, depicting the events of the Three Kingdoms period and shaping popular perception of the era.

18. Historical Perspectives and Controversies: Different interpretations and viewpoints among historians regarding the events, figures, and significance of the Three Kingdoms period, leading to ongoing debates and discussions.

19. Literary Influence: The impact of the Three Kingdoms period on Chinese literature, particularly through the epic novel "Romance of the Three Kingdoms," and its continued popularity and adaptation in various art forms.

20. Popular Perception: The general understanding, awareness, and perception of the Three Kingdoms era among the wider public, influenced by cultural adaptations, media portrayals, and popular culture.

Supplementary Materials

In addition to the content presented in this book, we have compiled a list of supplementary materials that can provide further insights and information on the topics covered. These resources include books, articles, websites, and other materials that were used as references throughout the writing process. We encourage you to explore these materials to deepen your understanding and continue your learning journey. Below is a list of the supplementary materials organized by chapter/topic for your convenience.

Introduction

Roberts, J. A. G. (1999). A Concise History of China. Harvard University Press.

Rafe, D. F. (2003). The Heritage of Han: The Impact of the Han Dynasty on the Formation of Modern China. EastBridge.

Chapter 1: The Fragmented Empire

de Crespigny, R. (2010). Imperial Warlord: A Biography of Cao Cao 155-220 AD. Brill.

Bielenstein, H. (1980). The Bureaucracy of Han Times. Cambridge University Press.

Chapter 2: Cao Cao and the Kingdom of Wei

Pei, S. (1977). The Chronicle of the Three Kingdoms. Harvard University Press.

de Crespigny, R. (2007). A Biographical Dictionary of Later Han to the Three Kingdoms (23-220 AD). Brill.
Chapter 3: Liu Bei and the Kingdom of Shu
Luo, G. (1995). Romance of the Three Kingdoms. Tuttle Publishing.
Roberts, M. (2001). The Three Kingdoms: A Historical Novel. University of California Press.
Chapter 4: Sun Quan and the Kingdom of Wu
Sun, Q. (2009). Sun Quan: The Emperor of Wu. Sichuan Publishing Group.
Wakeman, F. (1997). The Great Enterprise: The Manchu Reconstruction of Imperial Order in Seventeenth-century China. University of California Press.
Chapter 5: Alliances and Betrayals
Roberts, M. T. (2002). Shu, Wei, and Wu: A Study of the Three Kingdoms in Chinese Literature. The Chinese University Press.
Pei, S. (1977). The Chronicle of the Three Kingdoms. Harvard University Press.
Chapter 6: The Final Struggle for Supremacy
de Crespigny, R. (2004). Generals of the South: The Foundation and Early History of the Three Kingdoms State of Wu. Australian National University Press.

Ruan, F. (2015). Wu Kingdom's Campaigns Against Wei. Shanghai Ancient Books Publishing House.

Chapter 7: Legacy and Aftermath

Xu, Z. (2012). The Three Kingdoms Era and Its Characters. Shanghai People's Publishing House.

Saeki, A. (2011). Three Kingdoms and Chinese Culture. Shanghai Bookstore Publishing House.

Conclusion

Hinsch, B. (2011). The Conquest of the Han: The Emergence of a Chinese Empire. University of Michigan Press.

Dardess, J. W. (2010). A Short History of China: From Ancient Dynasties to Economic Powerhouse. Tuttle Publishing.